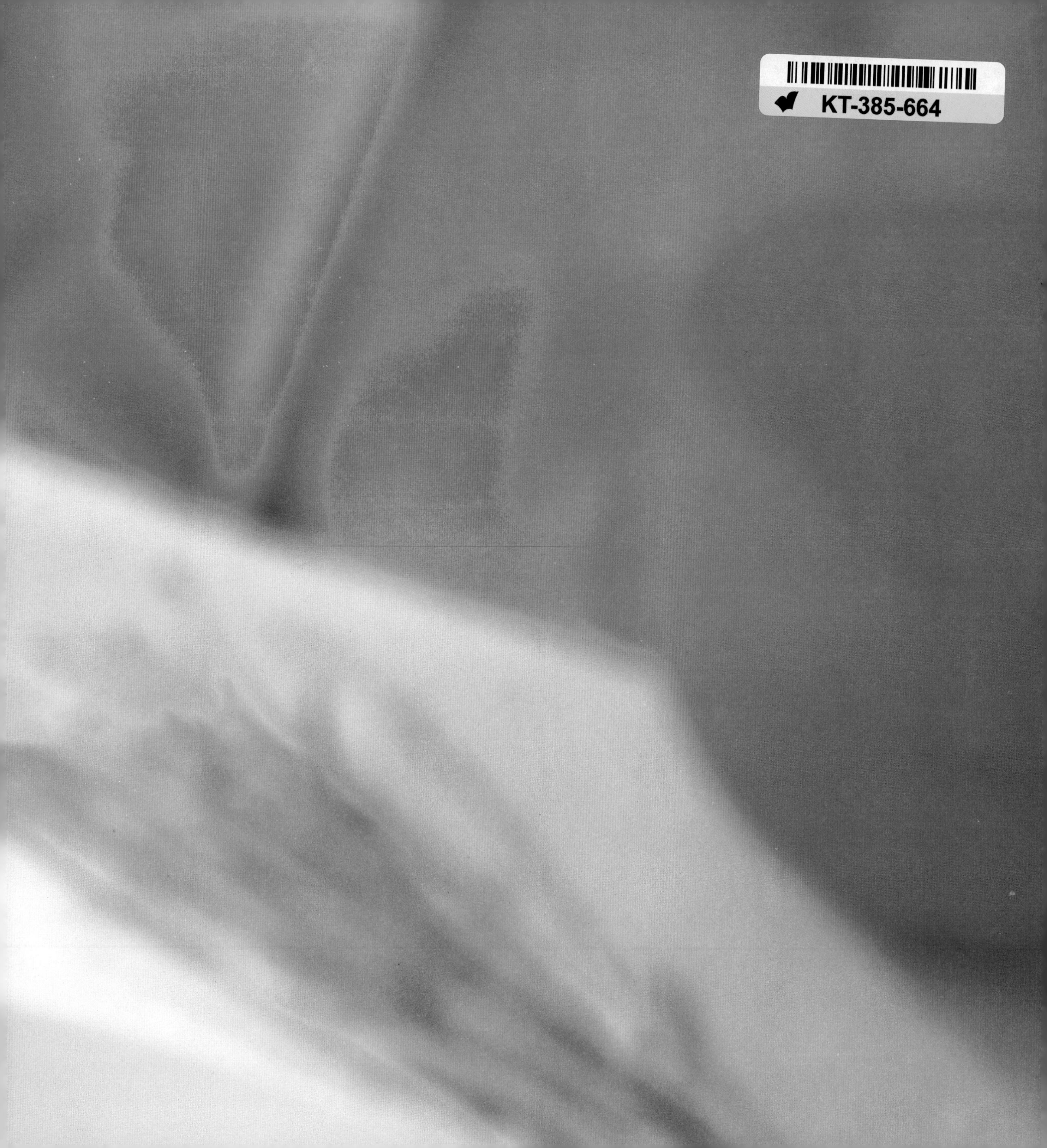

# Pasta

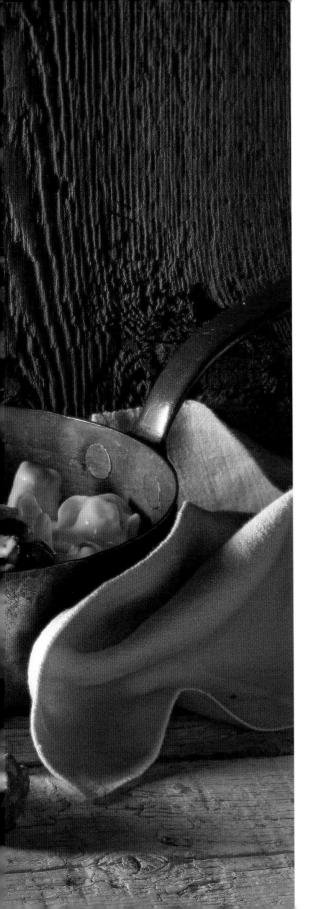

# Pasta

Sally Mansfield

hamlyn

Published in the UK in 1996
by Hamlyn, a division of Octopus Publishing Group Ltd
2–4 Heron Quays, London E14 4JP

This edition published 2001

ISBN 0 600 60571 X

Printed in China

NOTES

Both metric and imperial measurements have been given in all
recipes. Use one set of measurements only and not a mixture of
both.

Standard level spoon measurements are used in all recipes.
1 tablespoon = one 15 ml spoon
1 teaspoon = one 5 ml spoon

Eggs should be size 3 unless otherwise stated.

Milk should be full fat unless otherwise stated.

Pepper should be freshly ground black pepper unless otherwise
stated.

Fresh herbs should be used, unless otherwise stated. If
unavailable, use dried herbs as an alternative but halve the
quantities stated.

Measurements for canned food have been given as a standard
metric equivalent.

Ovens should be preheated to the specified temperature – if
using a fan-assisted oven, follow the manufacturer's instructions
for adjusting the time and the temperature.

Vegetarians should look for the 'V' symbol on a cheese to ensure
it is made with vegetarian rennet. There are vegetarian forms of
Parmesan, Feta, Cheddar, Cheshire, Red Leicester, dolcelatte
and many goats' cheeses, among others.

# Contents

# Introduction

Pasta has to be the world's ultimate convenience food. It is quick and easy to prepare, absolutely delicious and extremely cheap. You can, of course, buy it fresh now, or make it yourself, but as any discerning Italian cook will tell you, dried pasta is just as good if not better.

If cooking with pasta is new to you, you are sure to find all the recipes in this book easy to cook. The preparation time takes into account assembling the ingredients and any advance preparation such as chopping or slicing, plus any cooking which is incidental to the main cooking time – such as when sauces are cooked before a dish, like lasagne, can be assembled and baked. In simpler dishes, most of the sauces will be ready by the time the pasta has cooked.

This book includes chapters on soups, sauces to serve with pasta, meat, fish, salads, and vegetarian or meat-free dishes with pasta.

Most of the recipes will serve four, but it is a simple matter to halve the recipe to serve two. When cooking for crowds, you simply double the ingredients – you won't need to make too many adjustments.

Once you have tried these recipes, they are sure to become firm family favourites.

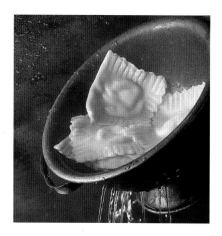

## COOKING PASTA

When some Italians are taught to cook pasta, they are told to take a strand of the cooked pasta out of the saucepan and hurl it against the wall. If it sticks, it is ready!

We are not recommending you do that, although it really can be a good indicator. A less messy but equally reliable test is to take a piece of cooked pasta from the pan and squeeze it between your fingers. If it breaks cleanly, it is cooked. Test the pasta frequently while it is cooking and make sure you don't overcook it; sticky, soggy pasta has little to commend it.

In fact, most of the recipes suggest that the dried pasta be cooked for between 8–12 minutes, but always check the packet instructions as the brand you have bought may have different cooking times.

Fresh pasta takes much less time to cook than dried, and this kind is ready when it rises to the surface of the boiling water in which it has been cooked.

Most of the recipes in this book use dried pasta, but there is also a chapter on how to make your own. For those who have the time, and fancy having a go, it can be very satisfying, not only because it tastes good, but also because it gives you a great sense of achievement.

## PASTA AND YOUR HEALTH

*Until very recent times, pasta was regarded as fattening, but this is by no means true. Pasta is made up largely of carbohydrate, with virtually no fat, so you fill up quickly without the high calorie intake. It is, in fact, a high-energy food, beloved of athletes.*

For an even higher fibre content, you can use wholewheat pasta. Although only a few of the recipes in this book actually specifically state that this type of pasta should be used, it can very easily be substituted for any of the plain varieties of pasta. Wholewheat pasta may absorb more water during cooking, however, so do remember to check it frequently.

## HOMEMADE PASTA

'Pasta' actually means 'paste' or 'dough', and is made from durum (hard) wheat ground to a coarse semolina and mixed with water.

However, because durum wheat flour is very hard, the dough can be difficult to work with, and so home-made pasta is usually easier to make if you use a mixture of flours. Once the dough is mixed, the true artistry and skill of the accomplished pasta maker comes into play.

Pasta is not at all difficult to make yourself. Follow these easy directions for making the dough, rolling it out with a rolling pin and cutting it to the required shape.

**1** Sift the flour and salt on to a clean dry work surface, heaping the flour high around the edges to create a well in the middle. Pour the eggs, oil and liquid flavourings (if any) into the central well.

**2** Using your fingers, gradually work all the dry ingredients into the egg mixture, being careful to prevent any of the liquids from spilling over the edges of the flour.

**3** When all the flour has been mixed thoroughly into the liquid ingredients, knead the dough for 10 minutes, or until it is smooth and elastic. Place the dough in a plastic bag and leave to rest for 30 minutes. This allows the gluten in the flour to become elastic.

**4** Roll out the dough on to a lightly floured surface as thinly as possible without tearing it (you should be able to see through the pasta). To turn the dough, roll it lightly over the rolling pin, as shown below. You could use a pasta machine to roll out and cut the dough, if you have one.

**5** Using a sharp knife, cut the pasta dough into strips to make tagliatelle, as shown above right, or roll into a tube and cut crossways. You can also

make many other pasta shapes – cut into big rectangular sheets for lasagne, or into squares in preparation for stuffed ravioli.

**6** Homemade pasta should be left to dry for about 10 minutes before cooking. Spread it out on a clean tea towel, or hang it over an improvised 'clothes-horse' to dry.

**7** When cooking fresh pasta, always allow at least 1.8–3.5 litres/3–6 pints water to 300 g/10 oz pasta. Use a large pasta pan or something the size of a pressure cooker to cook the pasta. Alternatively cook smaller batches in smaller pans. Give the pasta an occasional stir and partially cover the pan with a lid during the cooking time. The pasta is cooked when it rises to the top of the cooking liquid.

## FRESH PASTA

*Ready-made fresh pasta is widely available in supermarkets and delicatessens. Varieties such as tagliatelle and fettuccine are readily available, as are stuffed pastas such as tortellini and ravioli. Like homemade pasta, it cooks in a few minutes and is ready as soon as it rises to the surface of the boiling water.*

## DRIED PASTA

*This selection includes just a few of the varieties of pasta that are readily available in dried form. In general, the large shell shapes are meant to take stuffings, while hollow and ridged shapes are designed to hold as much sauce as possible.*

SPAGHETTI (STRING LIKE):
Available in various lengths, this long tubular pasta is now made in verdi, quick-cook, wholewheat and chilli and garlic varieties.

FARFALLE (BUTTERFLIES):
A double-ended pasta bow with the pasta pinched together in the centre, available in different sizes.

FUSILLI (CORKSCREW):
Pasta that has been twisted at the manufacturing stage.

TAGLIATELLE (FLAT RIBBON):
This pasta is rolled and cut into thin strips and is technically a noodle made from egg pasta.

PAPPARDELLE (BROAD NOODLES):
Egg noodles which are made in a similar way to tagliatelle, but cut into wider strips.

PENNE (QUILLS):
A tubular macaroni pasta made in various sizes, ribbed or plain.

CONCHIGLIE (SHELLS):
This pasta is produced in many different sizes and can be ribbed or plain. Conchigliette rigate is the name given to a small ridged version.

CAPPELLETTI (PEAKED HATS):
As the name suggests, this pasta resembles small hats. It is made in a variety of sizes and can be either ribbed or plain.

ZITO COL BUCO (WIDE TUBE):
This is a wide tubular pasta, which is really only ever made plain.

VERMICELLI (LITTLE WORMS):
Although the literal translation of the name may be a bit off-putting, this fine pasta, often sold in little nests or clusters, is delicious with almost any kind of sauce.

Other types of dried pasta used in this book include lumaconi (big snails), laganele, macaroni, tripolini, ruote (pasta wheels), bucato, tronchetti, spirals, twists and shells, angel hair, cannelloni and lasagne, including the convenient no-pre-cook kind. Also available are tricolore and multi-coloured pastas, and others flavoured with garlic, chilli or herbs.

However, do not worry if you can't find the precise pasta shape mentioned in the recipe. Simply substitute whichever kind is most easily available or whichever type you prefer.

## COOKING TIPS

*Both fresh and dried pasta must be one of the easiest foods to cook, but these simple tips will help you turn out perfectly cooked pasta every time.*

**1** Always bring the saucepan of water to a fast, rolling boil. Add a generous teaspoon or two of salt and a dash of oil. You can never season pasta satisfactorily after it has been cooked, so always salt the water before adding the pasta. The oil helps to separate the pasta and prevents the strands or shapes from sticking to each other. Always give the pasta a good stir once it has started cooking, though, as this helps to keep the pasta separate.

**2** When cooking spaghetti, add it all to the pan at the same time, gently pushing the pasta into the boiling water as it softens.

**3** Adjust the temperature under the pan after the pasta has been added, maintaining it at a steady boil but making sure that the water does not boil over.

**4** When it comes to how much pasta you need per person, it really is up to the individual. However, it is usual to allow between 50–125 g/2–4 oz each. It depends upon whether the pasta will be served simply or with a substantial sauce. When in doubt it is usually better to cook less rather than more, in order to maintain the balance of pasta to sauce.

## USEFUL EQUIPMENT

*You don't need to go out and buy any new equipment for successful pasta results – but there are a few items which are really useful and can make life a little easier when cooking pasta.*

SAUCEPAN
A really large saucepan is ideal –

preferably a straight-sided stainless steel pan that can hold up to 4 litres/ 7 pints of liquid.

### COLANDER

Cooked dry pasta swells to almost double its original bulk during cooking. So when it comes to straining, don't try using a small sieve. Use a large stainless steel colander – and choose one with a long handle, as the water will be boiling hot.

### PASTA FORK

To separate cooked pasta strands, a pasta fork or spoon is really one of the essential pieces of equipment. Stainless steel is preferable, but wood is fine too.

## IMPORTANT INGREDIENTS

*The ingredients used in this book are widely available, so you should be able to find all you need to recreate the recipes. If you do have problems for some reason, don't worry – substitute. If a recipe calls for sun-dried tomatoes and these are unobtainable, you can use fresh ripe ones with some tomato purée for extra flavour.*

### TOMATOES

Italy has perfect weather conditions for growing beautifully sweet, fruity plum tomatoes. Sadly this is not always the case in England, although naturally ripened tomatoes do taste wonderful in September, so use good-quality canned tomatoes instead. The canners harvest them when they are at their best, and the results can be excellent. Try out a variety of brands, as they can vary quite dramatically.

### OLIVE OIL

There's no substitute for good olive oil. The best is made from the first pressing of the olives – extra virgin olive oil. It is a golden-green colour and very rich in taste, and sadly very expensive too. When cooking and serving pasta without a sauce, it is worth using the best olive oil you can buy. Some say the finest olive oils come from the South of France, but Italian, Greek and Cyprus oils are all excellent. Don't be tempted to store olive oil in the refrigerator, as it will become thick and cloudy. Keep it on the shelf out of direct sunlight, but not too near the hob, as oil will become rancid if exposed to too much heat.

### ONIONS

Onions play a fundamental role in all nations' cuisines. Always choose firm ones with a pale papery skin, and avoid any that are soft or bruised. Ideally, keep onions in a cool, dark place to prevent sprouting.

Spanish onions are mild – ideal for those dishes where a delicate, rather than a robust, flavour is required.

Red-skinned onions are used in some recipes. They not only look wonderful, with their deep red layers of flesh, but also have a sweet mild flavour, which makes them perfect to eat raw in salads.

Shallots are widely used in French cooking. They have a deep russet papery skin and look more like a garlic bulb than an onion. They have a mild yet concentrated flavour.

### GARLIC

Garlic is highly favoured for its aromatic flavour and it has been used throughout the book. If you and your family prefer not to eat garlic, don't worry – it can quite easily be omitted from the recipes.

These days garlic is sold in many forms. For convenience both purée and fresh cloves have been used. Garlic purée is available in supermarkets and is usually stocked alongside the tomato purée. A general rule of thumb when using it is to substitute about 1 teaspoon of the purée for every 2 crushed garlic cloves.

Jars of minced garlic, preserved in a little vinegar and salt, are also available. Use minced garlic very sparingly as the flavour is much more concentrated than that of garlic purée or fresh crushed garlic.

### HERBS

Finding fresh herbs shouldn't be a problem, as they are now widely available all year round. Dried basil is no substitute for fresh, and this can be a bit difficult to track down during the winter months. To make sure you have fresh herbs available, you can freeze them throughout the summer when they are in abundance. If you do need to use dried herbs, always buy the freeze-dried varieties. These have a fresher flavour and a much better texture after cooking than herbs that are dried conventionally.

# Homemade Pasta

## Mushroom and Boursin Tagliatelle

PASTA:

250 g/8 oz strong white bread flour

2 eggs, beaten

1 tablespoon olive oil

50 g/2 oz frozen chopped spinach, thawed

SAUCE:

1 tablespoon olive oil

1 onion, chopped

2 garlic cloves, crushed

2 tablespoons snipped fresh chives

250 g/8 oz button mushrooms, sliced

125 ml/4 fl oz dry white wine

50 g/2 oz Boursin cheese with pepper

125 ml/4 fl oz double cream

salt and pepper

**1** Make the pasta as described on page 7, cut into strips to make tagliatelle.
**2** Bring at least 1.8 litres/3 pints water to the boil in a large pan. Add a dash of oil and a pinch of salt. Cook the pasta for 4 minutes.
**3** Heat the remaining oil in a pan and fry the onion and garlic until softened. Add half the chives with the mushrooms and wine. Bring to the boil and cook for 2 minutes, then stir in the Boursin and cream. Season with pepper. Stir until heated through.
**3** Drain the pasta, add to the pan and toss. Serve garnished with the remaining chives.

**Serves 4**
Preparation time: 30 minutes, plus 30 minutes resting time
Cooking time: 10 minutes

# Gnocchi in Herb Butter

Gnocchi is one of the easiest forms of pasta to make, and this sauce of garlic butter and herbs is perfect.

- 350 g/12 oz Cyprus potatoes, peeled
- 1 egg yolk, beaten
- 125 g/4 oz plain flour, sifted
- oil, see method
- 50 g/2 oz butter
- 1 teaspoon garlic purée
- 2 tablespoons chopped fresh parsley
- salt and pepper
- 50 g/2 oz Parmesan cheese, grated, to serve

**1** Cook the potatoes in a saucepan of boiling water for 30 minutes or until tender enough to mash. Drain well and return to the pan. Mash the potatoes, then return the pan to a very low heat to allow any excess liquid to evaporate.

**2** Beat in the egg yolk and flour until smooth, then turn the potato mixture out on to a floured work surface. Shape the potato mixture into walnut-sized balls.

**3** Flour a long pronged fork and carefully push a small ball of the paste on to the prongs. Using your second and forefinger drag the gnocchi paste up towards you. It should curl, leaving an impression on the underside. If the paste sticks, flour the fork again and don't push so hard. Dust the gnocchi with flour.

**4** Bring at least 1.8 litres/3 pints water to the boil in a large pan. Add a dash of oil and a pinch of salt. Cook the gnocchi in the boiling water, in 2 batches if necessary, for 3 minutes or until they all start to float to the surface. Drain well and keep hot.

**5** Melt the butter in a small frying pan and stir in the garlic purée and chopped parsley. Season to taste, and heat gently. Divide the gnocchi between 4 heated serving plates, pour over the butter mixture and toss lightly. Serve, accompanied by the grated Parmesan cheese.

**Serves 4**
Preparation time: 45 minutes
Cooking time: 3–6 minutes

# Beef Ravioli

Large, easy-to-handle ravioli.

PASTA:

- 250 g/8 oz strong white bread flour
- ½ teaspoon salt
- 2 eggs, beaten
- 2 tablespoons olive oil
- 6 tablespoons water

FILLING:

- 125 g/4 oz cold roast beef
- 125 g/4 oz fresh spinach, washed
- 1 onion, grated
- 1 garlic clove, crushed
- 2 tablespoons passata (sieved tomatoes)
- 1 egg, beaten
- 125 g/4 oz firm ricotta cheese, cubed
- salt and pepper
- basil sprigs, to garnish

**1** Make the pasta dough, as described on page 7, up to step 3.
**2** Make the filling. Mince the roast beef finely in a food processor. Cook the spinach in a saucepan with just the water that clings to the leaves after rinsing, until wilted. Drain, pressing the leaves against the colander to remove all excess liquid. Add to the minced beef with the onion, garlic and passata. Add salt and pepper to taste and process for 30 seconds more.
**3** On a lightly floured surface, roll out the dough as thinly as possible without tearing it (you should be able to see through the pasta).
**4** With a crimped pastry wheel, cut twenty-four 15 x 10 cm/6 x 4 inch rectangles. Brush one-half of each rectangle with the beaten egg and place a teaspoon of meat filling on each unglazed half. Place a cube of ricotta cheese on top of the filling and fold the pasta over. Seal the edges with a fork. Fill all the remaining pasta rectangles in exactly the same way. Set aside.
**5** Bring at least 1.8 litres/3 pints water to the boil in a large saucepan. Add a dash of oil and a generous pinch of salt. Cook the pasta, in batches if necessary, for 4–6 minutes. Drain thoroughly, tip the ravioli into a bowl and serve with plenty of black pepper, a little olive oil and a garnish of basil sprigs.

**Serves 4**
Preparation time: 45 minutes, plus 30 minutes resting time
Cooking time: 4–6 minutes

# Spinach Cannelloni

### PASTA:

- 250 g/8 oz strong white bread flour
- ½ teaspoon salt
- 2 eggs, beaten
- 1 tablespoon olive oil
- 50 g/2 oz frozen chopped spinach, thawed

### FILLING:

- 375 g/12 oz ricotta cheese
- 125 g/4 oz frozen chopped spinach, thawed
- 1 egg, beaten
- 25 g/1 oz plain flour
- 2 tablespoons garlic purée
- salt and pepper

### SAUCE AND TOPPING:

- 1 tablespoon olive oil
- 1 onion, chopped
- 1 x 550 g/18 oz jar passata
- 2 tablespoons mixed dried herbs
- 250 g/8 oz mozzarella cheese, grated

**1** Make the pasta. Sift the flour and salt on to a clean, dry work surface, heaping the flour high around the edges to create a well in the middle. Mix the eggs, oil and spinach in a small bowl. Carefully add the mixture to the well. Gradually work the flour into the egg mixture with your fingers (trying to prevent the liquids from spilling over the edges).

**2** Once all the flour has been incorporated, knead the dough for about 10 minutes, adding a little more flour if necessary. Place the dough in a plastic bag for about 30 minutes to rest.

**3** Make the filling. Mix the ricotta, spinach, egg, flour and garlic purée in a bowl. Add salt and pepper to taste. Spoon into a piping bag fitted with a large plain nozzle. Set aside.

**4** Make the sauce. Heat the oil in a pan and fry the onion until softened. Stir in the passata and herbs, and simmer for 5 minutes.

**5** Roll out the dough on a lightly floured surface as thinly as possible without tearing it. Cut into twelve 15 x 10 cm/6 x 4 inch sheets. Bring 1.8 litres/3 pints water to the boil. Add a dash of oil and a pinch of salt. Cook the pasta, in 2 batches if necessary, for 4 minutes.

**6** Remove the pasta with a slotted spoon and drain on paper towels. Pipe the filling along the width of each pasta sheet then roll them up to make filled cannelloni tubes.

**7** Arrange the tubes on the base of a lightly greased 1.8 litre/3 pint rectangular ovenproof dish. Pour the sauce over and top with the grated mozzarella. Bake in a preheated oven, 190°C (375°F), Gas Mark 5, for 45 minutes.

**Serves 4**
Preparation time: 45 minutes, plus 30 minutes resting time
Cooking time: 45 minutes
Oven temperature: 190°C (375°F), Gas Mark 5

# No Fuss Lasagne

This recipe is called 'no fuss lasagne' because it does not require special pasta-making equipment or complicated cooking arrangements. While the pasta dough is resting, you can save time by getting on with making the meat filling and the cheese sauce.

PASTA:
- 200 g/7 oz strong white bread flour
- ½ teaspoon salt
- 2 eggs, beaten
- 1 tablespoon olive oil

FILLING:
- 1 tablespoon olive oil
- 1 onion, chopped finely
- 1 tablespoon garlic purée
- 375 g/12 oz lean minced beef
- 4 tablespoons tomato purée
- 1 x 425 g/14 oz can plum tomatoes
- 1 beef stock cube, crumbled
- 2 tablespoons mixed dried herbs

SAUCE:
- 40 g/1½ oz butter
- 40 g/1½ oz plain flour
- 450 ml/¾ pint milk
- 250 g/8 oz Cheddar cheese or Pecorino cheese, grated
- salt and pepper

**1** Make the pasta as described on page 7, up to step 3. Leave to rest.
**2** Meanwhile, make the filling. Heat the oil in a saucepan and add the onion. Stir in the garlic purée. Fry for 3 minutes until the onion is softened. Add the remaining filling ingredients, stir well and simmer, uncovered, for

35 minutes until the mixture has thickened and reduced slightly.
**3** Make the sauce. Melt the butter in a saucepan. Stir in the flour and cook for 1 minute. Add the milk gradually, whisking or beating the sauce over a moderate heat until thickened. Season to taste. Beat in half the cheese, then cover the sauce closely and set aside.
**4** On a lightly floured surface, roll out the pasta as thinly as possible without breaking it (you should be able to see through the pasta). Cut the pasta into eight sheets, each 16 x 10 cm/ 6½ x 4 inches.
**5** Bring at least 1.8 litres/3 pints water to the boil in a large saucepan. Add a dash of oil and a generous pinch of salt. Cook the lasagne sheets, in 2 batches if necessary, for 2 minutes.

**6** Remove the pasta with a slotted spoon; drain on paper towels. Lay 2 sheets in the base of a lightly greased 1.8 litre/3 pint ovenproof dish. Spoon over one-third of the mince filling followed by one-third of the sauce. Continue layering the ingredients in this manner, using 3 sheets of lasagne for each of the following pasta layers, finishing with cheese sauce. Scatter the remaining cheese on top.
**7** Bake in a preheated oven, 190°C (375°F), Gas Mark 5, for about 35–45 minutes until golden.

**Serves 4**
Preparation time: 45 minutes, plus 30 minutes resting time
Cooking time: 55 minutes
Oven temperature: 190°C (375°F), Gas Mark 5

# Pasta
# Soups

## Tomato and Lentil Soup

50 g/2 oz red lentils

2 tablespoons olive oil

1 onion, chopped finely

2 spring onions, chopped

1 x 425 g/14 oz can plum tomatoes

2 tablepoons tomato purée

2 tablespoons chopped fresh mixed herbs

1.5 litres/2½ pints hot vegetable stock

75 g/3 oz dried mini pasta wheels

salt and pepper

grated Parmesan cheese, to garnish

**1** Cook the lentils in a saucepan of boiling water for 10 minutes; drain and set aside. Heat the oil in a large saucepan, add the onion and half the chopped spring onions and fry for 5 minutes or until softened.

**2** Add the lentils with the tomatoes, tomato purée and herbs. Pour in enough stock to cover. Bring to the boil, lower the heat and simmer for 30 minutes, adding more stock if necessary. Purée the soup in 2 batches in a blender or food processor until smooth.

**3** Return to a clean pan and stir in salt and pepper to taste. Add enough of the remaining stock to give the desired consistency. Bring to the boil, add the pasta, lower the heat and simmer for 8–12 minutes. Serve the soup in heated bowls, garnished with grated Parmesan cheese and the remaining spring onions.

**Serves 4**

Preparation time: 10 minutes

Cooking time: about 1 hour

# Spinach and Macaroni Soup

- 500 g/1 lb fresh spinach, washed
- 1 tablespoon ready-made pesto
- 900 ml/1½ pints hot chicken stock
- 125 g/4 oz quick-cook dried macaroni
- 1 teaspoon cornflour
- 150 ml/¼ pint double cream
- shavings of Parmesan cheese, to serve (optional)

**1** Place the spinach in a large saucepan with just the water that clings to its leaves after rinsing. Cook, uncovered, for 10 minutes, shaking the pan frequently.

**2** Remove the pan form the heat, drain the spinach and chop it by hand, or in 2 batches in a food processor for 30 seconds each or until smooth.

**3** Return the spinach to the clean saucepan, add the pesto and stir in the stock. Bring to the boil, add the pasta, lower the heat and simmer for 10 minutes.

**4** Mix the cornflour in a cup with just enough water to form a smooth paste. Add to the soup and continue to simmer, stirring constantly for 5 minutes or until the soup has thickened. Stir in the double cream, heat through without boiling and serve at once. Top each portion of the soup with shavings of Parmesan cheese, if liked.

### Serves 4
Preparation time: 5–10 minutes
Cooking time: 25–30 minutes

# Main Meal Soup

- 1 tablespoon olive oil
- 1 garlic clove, crushed
- 2 onions, sliced into rings
- 1 teaspoon ground coriander
- 2 carrots, cut into thin sticks
- 125 g/4 oz cooked chicken breast, shredded
- 1 tablespoon tomato purée
- 1.2 litres/2 pints hot chicken stock
- 75 g/3 oz dried pasta shells
- 75 g/3 oz mozzarella cheese, cubed
- 2 tablespoons chopped fresh parsley
- 1 teaspoon cayenne pepper
- salt

**1** Heat the oil in a large saucepan and fry the garlic and onions for 2 minutes. Stir in the coriander, then add the carrots and chicken. Fry over a moderate heat for 3 minutes.

**2** Stir in the tomato purée and stock. Bring to the boil, add the pasta, lower the heat and simmer for 8 minutes. Stir well and add salt to taste.

**3** Add the mozzarella and parsley, stir well, then sprinkle with cayenne pepper. Serve in heated bowls, with crusty bread, if liked.

**Serves 4**
Preparation time: 15 minutes
Cooking time: 13 minutes

# Clam and Sweetcorn Chowder

- 175 g/6 oz fresh clams, cleaned, or 2 x 290 g/9½ oz cans baby clams in brine, drained
- 1 tablespoon olive oil
- 1 onion, chopped finely
- 1 teaspoon ground turmeric
- 1 teaspoon plain flour
- 50 g/2 oz drained canned sweetcorn niblets
- 900 ml/1½ pints hot vegetable or fish stock
- 50 g/2 oz dried vermicelli
- 4 tablespoons double cream
- salt and pepper
- a few sprigs of flat leaf parsley, to garnish

**1** If using fresh clams put them in a large saucepan with 2 tablespoons of water. Cover with a lid and cook for 8 minutes or until the shells have opened. Discard any clams with shells which remain shut. Drain the rest of the clams, and remove all but 8 from their shells. Set the clams in their shells aside for the garnish.

**2** Heat the oil in a large saucepan, add the onion and fry for 5 minutes or until softened. Stir in the turmeric and fry for 1 minute more.

**3** Stir in the flour and fry for about 1 minute, then remove the pan from the heat.

**4** Add the fresh or drained canned clams to the onion mixture with the sweetcorn, hot stock and pasta. Simmer for 8 minutes.

**5** Add salt and pepper to taste and stir in the double cream. Serve the soup in heated bowls, garnished with a few sprigs of flat leaf parsley and the reserved clams in their shells, if used.

## Serves 4
Preparation time: 20 minutes
Cooking time: 23 minutes

# Coconut Tortelloni Soup

- 1½ tablespoons olive oil
- 325 g/11 oz fresh tortelloni verde
- knob of butter
- 1 onion, sliced
- 2 garlic cloves, crushed
- 200 ml/7 fl oz carton creamed coconut milk
- 200 ml/7 fl oz milk
- 475 ml/16 fl oz vegetable stock
- 1 bunch fresh basil leaves
- 125 g/4 oz mozzarella cheese balls, halved
- salt and pepper
- Parmesan cheese, grated, to serve

**1** Bring at least 1.8 litres/3 pints of water to the boil in a large saucepan. Add half a tablespoon of the oil and a good pinch of salt. Cook the pasta for 10–12 minutes or according to the packet instructions.

**2** Meanwhile, heat the remaining oil and butter in a large saucepan and fry the onion and garlic for 5–10 minutes until softened but not over browned. Then cover the pan with a lid, allowing the mixture to sweat.

**3** Add the creamed coconut milk, milk, vegetable stock and half the basil. Transfer to a food processor and blend the onion and coconut mixture until smooth. Pour back into the saucepan. Season well with salt and pepper. Simmer for 5 minutes.

**4** Drain the pasta and add to the soup with the remaining basil and the mozzarella balls. Season again to taste and then serve with plenty of grated Parmesan cheese and crispy bread sticks.

**Serves 4**
Preparation time: 10 minutes
Cooking time: 16 minutes

**VARIATION**

# Tomato Tortelloni Soup

Omit the coconut milk and replace with a 500g/1lb jar passata (sieved tomatoes). Grate the cheese on to disks of French bread and grill. Lay on the soup before serving.

# Ten Minute Farmhouse Soup

This soup really does only take 10 minutes to cook and is so easy that it's ideal for a quick supper.

- 1 tablespoon olive oil
- 1 onion, chopped
- 2 tablespons dried parsley
- 250 g/8 oz frozen diced mixed vegetables
- 2 tablespoons tomato purée
- 1.2 litres/2 pints hot vegetable stock
- 50 g/2 oz dried conchiglie
- salt and pepper

**1** Heat the oil in a large saucepan and fry the onion, parsley and vegetables with the tomato purée for 2 minutes.
**2** Add the hot vegetable stock. Bring to the boil, add the pasta, lower the heat and simmer, covered, for about 8 minutes or until the pasta is cooked. Add plenty of salt and pepper to taste. Serve at once with some crusty bread.

**Serves 4**
Preparation time: 2–3 minutes
Cooking time: 10 minutes

# Winter Broth

- 1 tablespoon olive oil
- 1 large shallot, chopped finely
- 250 g/8 oz mixed vegetables, such as potatoes, carrots and leeks, chopped finely
- 2 tablespoons mixed dried herbs
- 125 g/4 oz lean minced beef
- 4 tablespoons tomato purée
- 1 tablespoon yeast extract
- 1 tablespoon Worcestershire sauce
- 1.2 litres/2 pints hot beef stock
- 75 g/3 oz dried pipe bucatini or macaroni
- salt and pepper
- 25 g/1 oz Cheddar cheese, grated, to serve

**1** Heat the olive oil in a large saucepan. Add the chopped shallot and mixed vegetables with the mixed dried herbs. Fry, stirring constantly, for 5 minutes until the vegetables are softened and lightly browned.
**2** Stir in the beef and fry for a further 15 minutes, stirring occasionally, until the meat has browned.
**3** Add the tomato purée, the yeast extract and Worcestershire sauce, stir well and cook over a low heat for about 2 minutes.
**4** Gradually add the stock and bring to the boil. Add the pasta, with salt and pepper to taste. Lower the heat and simmer for 20 minutes. Serve, sprinkled with the grated cheese.

### Serves 4–6
Preparation time: 20 minutes
Cooking time: 42 minutes

# Country Bean and Pasta Broth

- 75 g/3 oz dried country bean mix or
  25 g/1 oz each dried kidney beans,
  pinto beans and black-eyed beans
- 25 g/1 oz dried porcini mushrooms
- 1 tablespoon olive oil
- 2 shallots, chopped finely
- 2 garlic cloves, crushed

- 125 g/4 oz button mushrooms, diced
- 2 tablespoons chopped mixed
  fresh herbs
- 50 g/2 oz mini dried pasta shapes
- 1.2 litres/2 pints hot beef stock
- salt and pepper
- chopped mixed fresh herbs, to garnish

**1** Soak the beans overnight in cold water in a covered bowl.

**2** The next day, drain the beans and place them in a large saucepan with water to cover. Bring to the boil and boil vigorously for 10 minutes. Skim any scum off the surface of the liquid and reduce the heat. Simmer, covered, for 1 hour, or until all the beans are very tender.

**3** Place the dried mushrooms in a bowl, cover with boiling water and set aside for 15 minutes, then drain, and reserve the liquid.

**4** Heat the oil in a large saucepan and fry the shallots and garlic for 3 minutes. Add all the mushrooms; stir well. Add the herbs and pasta shapes.

**5** Drain the beans and add them to the saucepan with the hot stock, reserved mushroom liquid and salt and pepper to taste. Bring to the boil, lower the heat and simmer for about 12 minutes. Serve at once, sprinkled with chopped, mixed fresh herbs, to garnish.

**Serves 4**

Preparation time: 10 minutes plus overnight soaking
Cooking time: about 1¼ hours

# Minestrone

This hearty soup makes an ideal winter starter but would also be perfect for lunch.

- 1 tablespoon olive oil
- 1 garlic clove, crushed
- 1 onion, chopped finely
- 50 g/2 oz rindless streaky bacon, chopped
- 2 carrots, diced finely
- 1 small leek, sliced finely
- 1 x 425 g/14 oz can chopped tomatoes
- 2 tablespoons tomato purée
- 1 tablespoon mixed dried herbs
- 1.2 litres/2 pints hot beef stock
- 75 g/3 oz small dried pasta shells
- 1 tablespoon grated Parmesan cheese
- salt and pepper
- chopped parsley, to garnish

**1** Heat the oil in a large saucepan and add the garlic and onion. Fry for 3 minutes, stirring constantly until softened but not browned.

**2** Add the bacon, carrots, leek and chopped tomatoes. Cook over a moderate heat for 10 minutes, stirring occasionally until the vegetables have softened. Add the tomato purée and herbs; stir well.

**3** Gradually stir in the beef stock and pasta shells. Add plenty of salt and pepper. Bring to the boil, lower the heat and simmer for 20 minutes. Serve in heated bowls, sprinkled with Parmesan and garnished with parsley.

**Serves 4**
Preparation time: 15 minutes
Cooing time: 33 minutes

# Carrot and Coriander Noodle Soup

- 1 tablespoon vegetable oil
- 1 onion, chopped
- 750 g/1½ lb carrots, chopped finely
- 1 teaspoon ground coriander
- 150 ml/¼ pint orange juice
- 1 litre/1¾ pints hot vegetable stock
- 50 g/2 oz dried egg thread noodles
- 3 tablespoons chopped fresh coriander
- salt and pepper

**1** Heat the oil in a large saucepan and fry the onion for 3 minutes until softened. Add the carrots and stir in the coriander. Fry for 5 minutes, stirring occasionally. Add the orange juice and 900 ml/1½ pints of the stock. Bring to the boil, lower the heat and simmer, partially covered, for 30 minutes.

**2** Meanwhile, bring a large saucepan of water to the boil. Add the noodles, stir well and then cover. Remove from the heat and set aside for 6 minutes. Drain, then snip into 2.5 cm/1 inch lengths. Set the noodles aside.

**3** Purée the soup in batches in a blender or food processor. Return to the clean saucepan and add the noodles. Stir in a little more stock if necessary.

**4** Add the fresh coriander, with salt and pepper to taste. Simmer the soup for 1 minute or until heated through, then serve.

**Serves 4**
Preparation time: 10 minutes
Cooking time: about 40 minutes

# Pasta Sauces

## Olive Oil, Chilli and Garlic Spaghetti

This type of dried pasta hasn't been available for very long. When you first remove it from the packet, the pasta smells as though it is going to taste quite garlicky, but it is the chilli flavour that really comes through when cooked.

6 tablespoons olive oil
500 g/1 lb chilli and garlic spaghetti
1 teaspoon freshly ground black pepper
1 x 285 g/9½ oz jar antipasto pepperoni condiverdi
2 tablespoons chopped fresh parsley
125 g/4 oz Parmesan cheese, in one piece
salt and pepper

**1** Bring at least 1.8 litres/3 pints water to the boil in a large saucepan. Add a dash of oil and a generous pinch of salt. Cook the dried pasta for about 8–12 minutes, until just tender.

**2** Drain the pasta and return it to the clean pan. Add the black pepper, remaining olive oil, antipasto and parsley, with salt and pepper to taste. Stir well. Simmer for about 1 minute or until thoroughly heated through.

**3** Spoon the pasta on to heated plates. Using a potato peeler, pare shavings of Parmesan cheese over the pasta. Serve at once.

**Serves 4**
Preparation time: 10 minutes
Cooking time: 13 minutes

1 Place the onion and garlic in a large frying pan with the butter and plenty of salt and pepper. Cook over a low heat for about 10 minutes, until the onion rings are translucent but not browned.

2 Meanwhile, bring a saucepan of water to the boil. Make a cross at the base of each tomato and plunge them into the water for 30 seconds. Remove the tomatoes with a slotted spoon and plunge them into cold water. Drain and peel off the skins.

3 Cut the tomatoes in half and remove the seeds. Chop the flesh and add it to the onion mixture, with salt and pepper to taste. Simmer, covered, for 10 minutes. Stir in the parsley.

4 While the sauce is simmering, bring at least 1.8 litres/3 pints water to the boil in a large saucepan. Add a dash of oil and a generous pinch of salt. Cook the pasta for 8–12 minutes, until just tender. Drain, return to the clean saucepan, and add the butter tomato sauce. Toss together gently and serve, garnished with chopped fresh parsley.

**Serves 4**
Preparation time: 10 minutes
Cooking time: 20 minutes

# Butter Tomato Zitoni

- 1 onion, sliced into rings
- 2 garlic cloves, crushed
- 125 g/4 oz unsalted butter
- 1 kg/2 lb fresh plum tomatoes
- 2 tablespoons chopped fresh parsley, plus extra to garnish
- 300 g/10 oz dried zitoni or other pasta shapes
- oil, see method
- salt and pepper

# Fettuccine Alfredo

- oil, see method
- 300 g/10 oz dried fettuccine
- 25 g/1 oz butter
- 1 onion, chopped finely
- 3 garlic cloves, chopped finely
- 450 ml/¾ pint single cream
- ¼ teaspoon grated nutmeg
- 1 egg, beaten
- salt and pepper
- 50 g/2 oz Parmesan cheese, grated
- 1 tablespoon chopped fresh parsley, to garnish

**1** Bring at least 1.8 litres/3 pints water to the boil. Add a dash of oil and a generous pinch of salt. Cook the pasta for 8–12 minutes, until just tender.

**2** Meanwhile, melt the butter in a very large frying pan. Add the onion and garlic and fry over a high heat for 1 minute, stirring constantly.

**3** Warm the cream in a saucepan. Pour it over the onion mixture and add the nutmeg. Bring the mixture to the boil, add salt and pepper to taste, then remove from the heat.

**4** Drain the pasta and add it to the sauce in the frying pan. Push the pasta to one side of the pan, return the pan to the heat and beat in the egg. While the mixture is cooking over a low heat, add the Parmesan. Stir well and as soon as the cheese has melted, tip the fettuccine on to heated plates. Serve at once, garnished with the parsley.

**Serves 4**
Preparation time: 10 minutes
Cooking time: 15 minutes

# Farfalle alla Napoletana

- 2 tablespoons olive oil
- 1 onion, chopped
- 2 garlic cloves, crushed
- 2 carrots, chopped finely, blanched
- 2 red peppers, cored, deseeded and chopped finely
- 4 large tomatoes, chopped
- 150 ml/¼ pint red wine
- 1 x 425 g/14 oz can chopped tomatoes with herbs
- 375 g/12 oz dried farfalle
- salt and pepper
- 1 bunch of basil, to garnish

**1** Heat the oil in a large frying pan. Add the chopped onion and garlic and fry for about 3 minutes until softened but not coloured.

**2** Add the carrots and red peppers and fry for a further 3 minutes. Stir in the chopped fresh tomatoes with the red wine and canned tomatoes. Add salt and pepper to taste. Simmer, partially covered, for 15 minutes.

**3** Meanwhile, bring at least 1.8 litres/3 pints water to the boil in a large saucepan. Add a dash of oil and a generous pinch of salt. Cook the pasta for about 8–12 minutes, until just tender.

**4** Drain the pasta, tip it on to a heated large serving platter, and season with black pepper. Drizzle with a little more oil if you wish. Pour over the sauce. Shred the basil leaves and scatter them over the sauce, to garnish.

**Serves 4**
Preparation time: 15 minutes
Cooking time: 21 minutes

VARIATIONS

# Bacon and Sweetcorn Farfalle

Make the sauce as for the main recipe. Five minutes before the end of the cooking time add about 125 g/4 oz grilled rindless back bacon rashers, crumbled, with 125 g/4 oz sliced button mushrooms and 50 g/2 oz drained canned sweetcorn niblets. Serve the sauce over the cooked pasta as in the main recipe.

# Coriander and Sun-dried Tomato Farfalle

Make the sauce as for the main recipe, omitting the carrots and basil. Substitute 8 sliced, sun-dried tomatoes and scatter 4 tablespoons chopped coriander leaves over the sauce, to garnish.

1 Make the sauce. Melt the butter in a saucepan. Add the flour and cook for 1 minute. Add the milk gradually, whisking or beating the sauce over a moderate heat until thickened. Stir in the Gruyère cheese, with salt and pepper to taste. Set aside.

2 Chop both the button and chanterelle mushrooms finely. Melt the butter in a large saucepan; add the mushrooms and garlic, with salt and pepper to taste. Fry over a low heat for 5 minutes until the mushrooms have cooked down. Remove from the heat.

3 Bring at least 1.8 litres/3 pints water to the boil in a large saucepan. Add a dash of oil and a generous pinch of salt. Cook the pasta for 4–6 minutes, or until it rises to the surface of the boiling water.

4 Meanwhile, add the Gruyère sauce to the mushroom mixture. Stir in the cream and cook gently over a low heat for about 2 minutes until thoroughly heated through.

5 Drain the pasta and add to the sauce. Toss well to mix, and check the seasoning. Serve at once, garnished with flat leaf parsley.

**Serves 4**
Preparation time: 20 minutes
Cooking time: 16 minutes

# Mushroom Gruyère Melt

- 250 g/8 oz button mushrooms
- 125 g/4 oz chanterelle mushrooms
- 25 g/1 oz butter
- 2 garlic cloves, crushed
- oil, see method

- 300 g/10 oz fresh tortellini
- 4 tablespoons double cream
- flat leaf parsley, to garnish

SAUCE:

- 25 g/1 oz butter
- 25 g/1 oz plain flour
- 450 ml/¾ pint milk
- 75 g/3 oz Gruyère cheese, grated
- salt and pepper

# Spirale and Sun-dried Tomatoes

- 300 g/10 oz dried spirale
- 4 tablespoons olive oil
- 8 sun-dried tomatoes in olive oil, drained and chopped
- 1 garlic clove, crushed
- 125 g/4 oz button mushrooms, sliced
- 125 g/4 oz rindless back bacon, grilled
- 4 large sage leaves, torn
- salt and pepper

**1** Bring at least 1.8 litres/3 pints water to the boil in a large saucepan. Add a dash of oil and a generous pinch of salt. Cook the pasta for 8–12 minutes, until just tender.
**2** Meanwhile, put the sun-dried tomatoes in a large saucepan with the remaining olive oil, garlic and mushrooms. Add salt and pepper to taste. Fry for 2 minutes, stirring constantly. Crumble in the bacon and reheat for 1 minute.
**3** Drain the pasta and add it to the sauce, with the sage leaves. Spoon on to heated plates and serve, with crusty bread, if liked.

**Serves 4**
Preparation time: 10 minutes
Cooking time: 12 minutes

# Wholewheat Fusilli with Spinach Cheese Sauce

Wholewheat pasta contains more fibre, and has a wonderfully nutty taste. You can substitute it for plain pasta in most of the recipes in this book.

- 1 tablespoon olive oil
- 300 g/10 oz fresh wholewheat fusilli, or other short, ridged pasta, or plain pasta
- 250 g/8 oz fresh spinach, washed
- 2 garlic cloves, crushed
- ¼ teaspoon grated nutmeg
- 300 ml/½ pint single cream
- 250 g/8 oz mascarpone cheese
- salt and pepper
- toasted flaked almonds, to garnish

**1** Bring at least 1.8 litres/3 pints water to the boil in a large saucepan. Add a dash of oil and a generous pinch of salt. Cook the pasta for 4–6 minutes, or until it rises to the surface of the boiling water.

**2** Meanwhile, discard any tough stalks from the freshly washed spinach. Place the spinach leaves in a large saucepan with just the water that clings to the leaves. Cook the spinach for 5 minutes or until the leaves are just wilted.

**3** Remove from the heat, drain the spinach well and squeeze it between 2 plates to remove all the excess water. With a sharp knife, chop the spinach finely and set it aside for a little while.

**4** Heat the remaining oil in a large saucepan and fry the garlic over a low heat for 2 minutes until softened. Stir in the nutmeg, the cream and the mascarpone cheese. Add salt and pepper to taste, raise the heat and bring to just below boiling point. Add the spinach, stir and cook for about 1 minute.

**5** Drain the pasta and then add it to the spinach sauce. Toss well to mix and season again, if necessary. Serve at once, garnished with the toasted flaked almonds and accompanied by a mixed salad, if you wish.

**Serves 4**
Preparation time: 20 minutes
Cooking time: 9 minutes

1 Bring at least 1.8 litres/3 pints water to the boil in a large saucepan. Add a dash of oil and a generous pinch of salt. Cook the spaghetti for about 8–12 minutes, until just tender.

2 Meanwhile, heat the remaining oil and butter in a very large frying pan. Fry the onion and bacon pieces until crisp. Remove from the heat.

3 Drain the pasta. Pour a little of the oil from the bacon mixture into the clean pasta pan. Return the pasta to the pan and stir over a moderate heat for 1 minute. Add the bacon mixture and toss well. Make a slight dip in the centre and add the eggs, tossing the pasta constantly over the heat for 2 minutes or until the eggs have just cooked.

4 Set aside one-third of the grated Parmesan cheese. Add the rest, with the Pecorino cheese, to the pasta. Spoon the pasta on to heated plates, sprinkle with the reserved Parmesan and garnish with the chopped parsley.

**Serves 4**

Preparation time: 20 minutes
Cooking time: 15 minutes

# Spaghetti Carbonara

Many carbonara sauces are creamy, having been finished with lashings of double cream. Unusually, there is no cream included in this recipe but the eggs added at the end will give it a truly creamy flavour. Do not worry about using raw eggs: the hot pasta will cook the eggs just enough, while retaining their natural creaminess.

- 1 tablespoon olive oil
- pinch of salt
- 375 g/12 oz dried spaghetti
- 25 g/1 oz butter
- 1 onion, chopped
- 375 g/12 oz rindless smoked back bacon, chopped
- 4 eggs, beaten
- 75 g/3 oz Parmesan cheese, grated
- 125 g/4 oz Pecorino cheese, grated
- 1 tablespoon chopped fresh parsley, to garnish

# Four Herb Fusilli

Prosciutto is highly regarded air-dried Italian ham, which is usually served in very thin slices. The most well-known proscuitto comes from Parma and it is commonly known as Parma ham.

- 2 tablespoons olive oil
- 375 g/12 oz dried fusilli
- 2 spring onions, chopped finely
- 2 tablespoons chopped fresh parsley
- 2 tablespoons chopped fresh basil
- 2 tablespoons chopped fresh thyme
- 2 tablespoons chopped fresh coriander
- 4 slices prosciutto, chopped
- 300 ml/½ pint double cream or crème fraîche
- salt and pepper
- 2 tablespoons chopped mixed fresh coriander and thyme, to garnish

1 Bring at least 1.8 litres/3 pints water to the boil in a large saucepan. Add a dash of oil and a generous pinch of salt. Cook the pasta for 8–12 minutes, until just tender.
2 Three minutes before the end of the cooking time, heat the remaining olive oil in a saucepan. Add the spring onions and fry for 1 minute.
3 Stir in all the herbs, prosciutto and cream, with salt and pepper to taste. Simmer for 3 minutes. Drain the pasta and add to the sauce. Toss to mix. Serve garnished with the chopped fresh coriander and thyme.

**Serves 4**
Preparation time: 10 minutes
Cooking time: 12 minutes

# Tagliatelle with Chilli and Roast Cherry Tomato Dressing

- 250 g/8 oz cherry tomatoes
- sea salt
- 2 teaspoons ready-made pesto
- 4 tablespoons olive oil
- 2 spring onions, sliced finely
- 1 red or green chilli, seeded and finely chopped
- 2 garlic cloves, chopped
- 1 tablespoon raspberry vinegar
- 1 tablespoon orange juice
- 2 tablespoons toasted hazelnuts, chopped
- 2 tablespoons chopped fresh basil
- 500 g/1 lb fresh tagliatelle verdi
- salt and pepper

TO GARNISH:

- a few basil leaves
- Parmesan cheese, grated (optional)

**1** Halve the tomatoes and arrange on a baking sheet. Sprinkle with a little salt and top with pesto; carefully toss making sure you coat the tomatoes well. Cook in a preheated oven at 200°C (400°F), Gas Mark 6 for 15 minutes.

**2** Meanwhile, heat the olive oil in a small saucepan. Add the spring onions, chilli and garlic, fry for 1 minute, stirring continuously. Remove from the heat, add the vinegar, orange juice, hazelnuts and basil. Stir well, season and keep warm.

**3** Meanwhile, bring at least 1.8 litres/ 3 pints water to the boil in a large saucepan. Add a dash of oil and a generous pinch of salt. Just before the tomatoes are ready, cook the pasta for 4 minutes or according to the packet instructions. Drain the pasta and return it to the pan. Add the spring onion mixture, toss well. Carefully add the tomatoes along with all of the cooking juices.

**4** Serve garnished with basil and plenty of freshly grated Parmesan cheese, if you wish.

**Serves 4**

Preparation time: 10 minutes
Cooking time: 15 minutes
Oven temperature: 200°C (400°F), Gas Mark 6

VARIATION

Replace the raspberry vinegar with a little balsamic vinegar and omit the orange juice. Stir in 4 tablespoons of crème fraîche.

# Fettuccine with Spicy Tomato Sauce

- 2 tablespoons olive oil
- 300 g/10 oz dried fettuccine
- 3 garlic cloves, crushed
- 1 teaspoon mild chilli powder
- 1 teaspoon ground coriander
- 125 g/4 oz sliced pepperoni
- 1 x 425 g/14 oz can chopped tomatoes
- 6 tablespoons passata (sieved tomatoes)
- 4 tablespoons red wine
- 1 tablespoon basil leaves
- salt and pepper
- a few sprigs of thyme, to garnish

**1** Bring at least 1.8 litres/3 pints water to the boil in a large saucepan. Add a dash of oil and a generous pinch of salt. Cook the pasta for 8–12 minutes, until tender.
**2** Meanwhile, heat the remaining oil in a large frying pan. Add the garlic, chilli powder and coriander. Fry over a low to moderate heat for 1 minute, stirring constantly.

**3** Stir in the pepperoni, tomatoes toether with the pan juices, passata and red wine, with salt and pepper to taste. Simmer, uncovered, for about 10 minutes.
**4** Drain the pasta and add it to the sauce. Toss and season with more pepper, if liked. Add the basil and toss again to mix. Sprinkle with thyme to garnish. Serve while still piping hot.

### Serves 4
Preparation time: 10 minutes
Cooking time: 12 minutes

# Red Pesto with Spaghetti Verde

Plain spaghetti can be used in this recipe, but the colour of the spinach-flavoured variety makes it the perfect foil for the red pesto sauce.

- **2 tablespoons olive oil**
- **375 g/12 oz dried spaghetti verde**
- **3 garlic cloves, crushed**
- **6 tablespoons ready-made red pesto**
- **3 tablespoons orange juice or balsamic vinegar**
- **salt and pepper**

**1** Bring at least 1.8 litres/3 pints water to the boil in a large saucepan. Add a dash of oil and a generous pinch of salt. Cook the pasta for about 8–12 minutes, until just tender.
**2** Three minutes before the end of the cooking time, heat the remaining oil in a large frying pan. Add the garlic and fry for 2 minutes. Reduce the heat and stir in the pesto and orange juice or balsamic vinegar, and add salt and pepper to taste. Simmer for about 1 minute.
**3** Drain the pasta and add it to the sauce. Toss well, sprinkle with more black pepper and serve at once.

**Serves 4**
Preparation time: 7 minutes
Cooking time: 8–12 minutes

# Pasta with Meat

## Crispy Bacon Pappardelle

1 tablespoon olive oil

1 onion, sliced

125 g/4 oz chorizo (spicy Spanish) sausage, sliced

oil, see method

375 g/12 oz dried pappardelle or other broad egg noodles

2 large ripe tomatoes

1 tablespoon chopped fresh coriander

8 rindless unsmoked back bacon rashers, grilled and cut into strips

salt

a few coriander leaves, to garnish

**1** Heat the oil in a large pan, add the onion and fry for 5 minutes until softened but not coloured. Add the chorizo sausage and fry for 5 minutes more, stirring.

**2** Meanwhile, bring 1.8 litres/3 pints water to the boil in a saucepan. Add a dash of oil and a generous pinch of salt. Cook the pasta for 8–12 minutes, until just tender.

**3** While the pasta is cooking, prepare the tomatoes. Bring a saucepan of water to the boil. Make a cross at the base of each tomato and plunge them into the water for 30 seconds. Remove with a slotted spoon and plunge them into cold water. Drain and peel off the skins. Cut the tomatoes in half and remove the seeds. Chop the flesh into large chunks. Add it to the sausage mixture with the coriander. Fry for a further 5 minutes. Add the bacon.

**4** Drain the pasta, drizzle with a little oil and add to the sausage mixture. Stir and serve, garnished with coriander leaves.

**Serves 4**

Preparation time: 15 minutes

Cooking time: 25 minutes

# Lasagne

This is the sort of lasagne which is best eaten with a spoon. Serve good crusty bread to mop up the juices.

- 9 dried 'no pre-cook' lasagne sheets
- 50 g/2 oz Parmesan cheese, grated

MEAT SAUCE:
- 2 tablespoons olive oil
- 2 onions, chopped finely
- 3 garlic cloves, crushed
- 1 tablespoon dried oregano
- 1 tablespoon dried basil
- 3 tablespoons tomato purée
- 500 g/1 lb lean minced beef

- 1 x 425 g/14 oz can plum tomatoes
- salt and pepper

CHEESE SAUCE:
- 4 cloves
- 1 onion, halved
- 600 ml/1 pint skimmed milk
- 25 g/1 oz butter
- 25 g/1 oz plain flour
- 250 g/8 oz Cheddar cheese, grated

**1** Make the meat sauce. Heat the oil in a large saucepan and fry the onions for 3–5 minutes, until softened. Add the garlic and fry for 1 minute more, then stir in the herbs, tomato purée and beef. Fry the mixture, stirring constantly, for 5 minutes. Add the tomatoes with the can juices to the filling with salt and pepper to taste. Stir well. Cover the pan and simmer the meat sauce for 45 minutes, stirring occasionally.
**2** Meanwhile, infuse the milk for the cheese sauce. Stick the cloves in the onion halves and put them in a small saucepan. Add the milk and bring to just below boiling point. Remove the pan from the heat and set aside for 15 minutes. Remove the onion halves and cloves.
**3** Melt the butter in a saucepan. Stir in the flour and cook for 1 minute. Add the infused milk gradually, whisking or beating the sauce over a moderate heat until thickened. Add the Cheddar cheese, stir well until melted, then stir in salt and pepper to taste. Set aside.
**4** Grease the base and sides of an oval or rectangular 1.8 litre/3 pint ovenproof dish. Spoon one-third of the meat mixture over the base. Spread over a quarter of the cheese sauce and cover with 3 sheets of lasagne.
**5** Repeat the layering process twice more, finishing with a layer of pasta. Cover with the remaining cheese sauce. Sprinkle over the Parmesan. Bake the lasagne in a preheated oven, 190°C (375°F), Gas Mark 5, for 1 hour. Serve with a green salad and crusty bread.

**Serves 4**
Preparation time: 1 hour
Cooking time: 1 hour
Oven temperature: 190°C (375°F), Gas Mark 5

VARIATIONS

# Lasagne Verde

Replace the plain lasagne with the same quantity of lasagne verde (spinach-flavoured lasagne). Replace the tomato purée with the same quantity of ready-made pesto or 3 tablespoons chopped fresh basil. Proceed as for the main recipe.

# Chicken Lasagne

Replace the minced beef with the same quantity of lean minced chicken. Replace half the milk with natural yogurt when making the cheese sauce. Proceed as for the main recipe.

# Tagliatelle Bolognese

- 1 tablespoon olive oil
- 1 onion, chopped
- 2 garlic cloves, crushed
- 425 g/12 oz lean minced beef
- 2 tablespoons tomato purée
- 1 tablespoon chopped mixed fresh herbs
- 1 x 425 g/14 oz can chopped tomatoes
- 1 teaspoon Worcestershire sauce
- 150 ml/¼ pint hot beef stock
- oil, see method
- 375 g/12 oz dried tagliatelle, verde or plain
- salt and pepper
- basil leaves, to garnish

**1** Heat the oil in a large saucepan, add the onion and garlic and fry for 5 minutes until softened. Stir in the meat. Increase the heat and fry for 3 minutes, stirring constantly.

**2** Reduce the heat, add the tomato purée and herbs and stir well. Add the tomatoes with the can juices, and stir in the Worcestershire sauce and stock. Simmer, covered, for 1 hour, stirring occasionally, until the sauce is rich and thickened. Add salt and pepper to taste.

**3** About 10 minutes before the end of the cooking time, bring at least 1.8 litres/3 pints water to the boil in a large saucepan. Add a dash of oil and a generous pinch of salt. Cook the tagliatelle for 8–12 minutes, until just tender. Drain well, drizzle with a little more olive oil and season with black pepper.

**4** Place the pasta on serving plates and spoon the sauce over. Garnish with basil and serve. Good country bread and a mixed green salad are suitable accompaniments.

**Serves 4**
Preparation time: 30 minutes
Cooking time: about 1¼ hours

# Spicy Chicken Pipe Rigate

'Pipe' are curved elbow-shaped pasta shapes, and these have the ribbed or 'rigate' surface, which is designed to take up large quantities of sauce between the ribs. Pipe rigate are best suited to those sauces which contain chicken, meat, cheese and/or cream, or tomato.

- 1 teaspoon chilli powder
- 1 teaspoon cayenne pepper
- 1 teaspoon turmeric
- 1 tablespoon olive oil, plus a little extra
- 250 g/8 oz skinned chicken breast, cut into bite-sized pieces
- 1 onion, chopped
- 1 x 425 g/14 oz can plum tomatoes
- 1 teaspoon caster sugar
- 1 bunch of fresh basil
- 375 g/12 oz dried pipe rigate
- salt and pepper

**1** In a bowl, mix together the chilli powder, cayenne, turmeric and 1 teaspoon of the olive oil. Stir to form a paste. Add the chicken pieces and coat thoroughly in the spice mixture. Cover and set aside for 15 minutes.

**2** Meanwhile, heat the remaining olive oil in a large frying pan. Add the onion and fry for 3 minutes until softened but not coloured. Add the tomatoes with the can juices and the sugar. Strip the basil leaves from the stems. Set some leaves aside for the garnish. Chop the rest finely and add them to the pan. Boil the mixture rapidly for 5 minutes, stirring occasionally to break up the tomatoes.

**3** Bring 1.8 litres/3 pints water to the boil in a large saucepan. Add a dash of oil and a generous pinch of salt. Cook the pasta for about 8–12 minutes, until just tender.

**4** Meanwhile, dry-fry the spicy chicken pieces in a non-stick frying pan for 10 minutes or until crisp. Add to the sauce. Drain the pasta, drizzle with a little more oil and add salt and pepper. Arrange the pasta on a large serving platter and pour over the sauce. Serve garnished with the reserved basil leaves.

## Serves 4

Preparation time: 15 minutes, plus 15 minutes marinating time
Cooking time: 25–30 minutes

# Pork Schnitzels with Pappardelle

- 4 pork escalopes, about 125 g/4 oz each
- 1 egg
- 125 g/4 oz fresh white breadcrumbs
- 75 g/3 oz butter
- 2 tablespoons vegetable oil
- 250 g/8 oz dried pappardelle or other broad egg noodles
- olive oil, see method
- 50 g/2 oz anchovy fillets, chopped
- 150 ml/¼ pint double cream
- 2 tablespoons roughly chopped oregano
- salt and pepper

**1** Place the pork between 2 sheets of greaseproof paper and flatten with a meat mallet or rolling pin until double their original size.
**2** Beat the egg together with salt and pepper in a shallow bowl. Spread out the breadcrumbs on a sheet of foil. Dip each schnitzel in the egg, then coat in the breadcrumbs. Melt the butter with the oil in a large frying pan. Fry the schnitzels for 15 minutes, turning once.
**3** Meanwhile, bring at least 1.8 litres/3 pints water to the boil in a large saucepan. Add a dash of oil and a generous pinch of salt. Cook the pasta for about 8–12 minutes, until just tender.
**4** Remove the pork from the pan and drain on paper towels. Keep hot.
**5** Drain the pasta, and return it to the clean saucepan. Add the anchovies, cream and oregano. Toss well. Arrange the pasta on a large heated platter and serve with the schnitzels.

**Serves 4**
Preparation time: 20 minutes
Cooking time: 15 minutes

VARIATIONS

## Pork Schnitzels with Paprika Sauce

Cook the schnitzels and pasta as for the main recipe. Meanwhile, heat 1 tablespoon olive oil in a large frying pan. Add 1 red and 1 yellow pepper, (cored, seeded, and sliced into rings). Fry for 3 minutes. Stir in 1 teaspoon paprika and 150 ml/¼ pint passata (sieved tomatoes). Simmer the sauce for 10 minutes and toss with the pasta instead of adding the anchovies, cream and herbs. Serve at once with the schnitzels.

## Pork Schnitzels with Mushrooms

This is a variation on Pork Schnitzels with Paprika Sauce (above). Cook the schnitzels and pasta as before. Make the sauce, adding 15 g/½ oz butter when heating the oil in the frying pan. Add 125 g/4 oz sliced button mushrooms and 50 g/2 oz sliced shiitake mushrooms to the pepper mixture. Omit the paprika when adding the passata. Simmer the sauce for 10 minutes before tossing it with the pasta. Serve with the schnitzels.

# Smoked Chicken and Penne Rigate

- 1 tablespoon olive oil
- 375 g/12 oz dried penne rigate
- 2 shallots, chopped finely
- 125 g/4 oz chestnut mushrooms, sliced
- 2 x 80 g/3¼ oz packets Boursin cheese with herbs
- 150 ml/¼ pint double cream
- 250 g/8 oz smoked chicken breast, skinned and sliced
- 2 tablespoons chopped fresh parsley
- salt and pepper

**1** Bring at least 1.8 litres/3 pints water to the boil in a large saucepan. Add a dash of oil and a generous pinch of salt. Cook the pasta for 8–12 minutes, until just tender.

**2** Meanwhile, heat the remaining oil in a frying pan and add the shallots. Fry for 1 minute, stirring constantly, until softened. Add the mushrooms and fry for 2 minutes more.

**3** Reduce the heat and add the Boursin cheese, breaking it up with the back of a wooden spoon. Stir in the double cream.

**4** Add the chicken and parsley. Stir over a low heat for 5 minutes until thoroughly heated through. Add plenty of salt and pepper to taste.

**5** Drain the pasta and drizzle with a little oil. Season with black pepper and add to the sauce. Stir well and then serve.

**Serves 4**
Preparation time: 10 minutes
Cooking time: 12 minutes

# Chinese Beef Cappellini

- 4 sirloin steaks, about 125 g/4 oz each
- 1 tablespoon crushed red peppercorns
- 1 tablespoon mild chilli powder
- 1 tablespoon Szechuan powder
- 3 tablespoons light soy sauce
- 3 tablespoons dry sherry
- 2 teaspoons sesame or light vegetable oil
- 375 g/12 oz dried cappellini d'angelo (angel hair pasta)
- 1 bunch of spring onions, shredded
- 1 red pepper, cored, deseeded and sliced thinly
- 1 green pepper, cored, deseeded and sliced thinly
- salt

**1** Cut the steaks into 5 mm/¼ inch wide strips. In a shallow bowl mix together the red peppercorns, mild chilli powder, Szechuan powder, light soy sauce and sherry. Add the strips of steak to the marinade and toss to coat thoroughly.

**2** Bring at least 1.8 litres/3 pints water to the boil in a large saucepan. Add a dash of oil and a generous pinch of salt. Cook the pasta for 5–7 minutes, until just tender.

**3** Heat a wok or a very large frying pan. Add the remaining oil and heat until a blue haze can be seen. Set aside a few of the shredded spring onions for the garnish. Add the remainder to the wok or frying pan along with the sliced red and green peppers and stir-fry for 2 minutes. Then add the marinated beef, together with all of the marinade, and stir-fry for a further 5 minutes.

**4** Drain the pasta. Place on a large warmed serving platter and spoon the beef and pepper mixture over the top. Garnish the dish with the reserved shredded spring onions and serve immediately.

**Serves 4**
Preparation time: 10 minutes
Cooking time: 7 minutes

# Gnocchi Parma Bake

- 2½ tablespoons olive oil
- 1 red-skinned onion, halved and sliced
- 2 garlic cloves, crushed
- good pinch of dried tarragon
- 1 x 425 g/14 oz can tomatoes, drained
- 250 g/8 oz mascarpone cheese
- 2 dessertspoons sun-dried tomato sauce

- 325 g/11 oz fresh gnocchi
- 125 g/4 oz Cheddar cheese, grated
- 50 g/2 oz fresh white breadcrumbs
- 75 g/3 oz Parma ham
- 10 pitted green olives
- salt and pepper

**1** Heat 2 tablespoons of the oil and fry the onion and garlic for 5 minutes over a medium heat until softened. Add the tarragon.
**2** Put the drained tomatoes and mascarpone cheese in a food processor and blend until smooth.
**3** Stir the tomato sauce into the onion mixture, add the sun-dried tomato sauce and season well. Simmer gently.
**4** Meanwhile, bring at least 1.8 litres/3 pints water to the boil in a large saucepan. Add the remaining oil and a good pinch of salt. Cook the gnocchi for 1–2 minutes or until they rise to the surface.
**5** Drain and put in a large ovenproof dish. Pour the tomato sauce over. Stir the cheese and breadcrumbs together and scatter over the mixture.
**6** Tear the Parma ham into thin lengths and randomly lay over the topping. Scatter over the olives and season again. Sprinkle a little more tarragon on top.
**7** Cook in a preheated oven 180°C (350°F), Gas Mark 4, for 20–25 minutes or until the top is bubbling and golden. Serve with a lightly tossed salad.

**Serves 4**
Preparation time: 15 minutes
Cooking time: 20–25 minutes
Oven temperature: 180°C (350°F), Gas Mark 4

**VARIATION**

For a vegetarian alternative, omit the Parma ham and lay grilled slices of aubergine over the mixture before topping with the cheese and breadcrumbs.

# Mushroom and Kidney Turbigo with Pappardelle

- 2 tablespoons olive oil
- 25 g/1 oz butter
- 2 onions, sliced into rings
- 8 small chipolata sausages
- 2 tablespoons plain flour
- 3 tablespoons tomato purée
- 6 tablespoons red wine
- 150 ml/¼ pint hot lamb stock
- 125 g/4 oz button mushrooms, halved if large
- 500 g/1 lb lamb's kidneys
- 375 g/12 oz dried pappardelle or other broad egg noodles
- 150 ml/¼ pint double cream
- salt and pepper
- 1 tablespoon chopped fresh parsley, to garnish

**1** Heat half of the oil with half the butter in a large saucepan. Add the onions and chipolata sausages. Cook over a moderate heat for 10 minutes or until browned. Remove the sausages and set aside.

**2** Stir 1 tablespoon of the flour into the onion mixture; cook until golden. Stir in the tomato purée, red wine, hot lamb stock and mushrooms with salt and pepper to taste. Simmer, partially covered, for 10 minutes or until thickened.

**3** Meanwhile, halve the kidneys. Cut away the white core from the centre of each kidney. Toss the kidneys in the remaining plain flour in a strong polythene bag.

**4** Bring at least 1.8 litres/3 pints water to the boil in a large saucepan. Add a dash of oil and a generous pinch of salt. Cook the pasta for 8–12 minutes, until just tender.

**5** While the pasta is cooking, heat the remaining butter and oil in a large frying pan. Fry the kidneys for 6 minutes, turning constantly. Add to the onion sauce. Return the sausages to the pan and simmer for 5 minutes. Stir in the double cream and reheat without boiling.

**6** Drain the pasta and pile it on a large platter. Spoon over the sauce and garnish with the chopped parsley. Serve at once.

**Serves 4**
Preparation time: 45 minutes
Cooking time: 30–35 minutes

# Lamb's Liver with Spaghetti

- 1 tablespoon plain flour
- 1 teaspoon cayenne pepper
- 1 teaspoon freshly ground black pepper
- 1 teaspoon salt
- grated rind and juice of 1 lemon
- 500 g/1 lb lamb's liver, trimmed and sliced thinly
- 2 eggs
- 125 g/4 oz medium oatmeal
- 6 tablespoons light olive oil
- 375 g/12 oz dried tomato or plain spaghetti
- 2 tablespoons orange juice
- 1 spring onion, chopped finely
- 50 g/2 oz Parmesan cheese, to garnish

**1** Combine the flour, cayenne, black pepper and salt in a bowl. Grate the rind of the lemon in to the bowl. Mix well. Add the liver and coat each slice in the flour mixture.

**2** Beat the eggs in a shallow bowl. Spread out the oatmeal on a sheet of foil. Dip the liver slices in the beaten egg, then coat them in the oatmeal. Set aside.

**3** Bring at least 1.8 litres/3 pints water to the boil in a large saucepan. Add a dash of oil and a generous pinch of salt. Cook the pasta for 8–12 minutes, until just tender.

**4** Meanwhile, heat 2 tablespoons of the remaining oil in a large frying pan. Fry the coated lamb's liver slices over a high heat for 4 minutes on each side. Drain well on kitchen paper and keep hot.

**5** Drain the pasta, return it to the clean saucepan and pour over the remaining olive oil. Add the lemon juice and orange juice and toss lightly. Place the dressed pasta on a large platter and arrange the lamb's liver on top. Sprinkle with the finely chopped spring onion, garnish with shavings of Parmesan and serve.

## Serves 4

Preparation time: 30 minutes
Cooking time: 12 minutes

# Pasta with Fish

## Spaghetti Marinara

The wine and stock in the velouté sauce gives this dish
a dinner party feel. You can use milk instead of wine if you prefer.

oil, see method
300 g/10 oz dried spaghetti
25 g/1 oz butter
25 g/1 oz plain flour
125 ml/4 fl oz dry white wine
125 ml/4 fl oz hot vegetable stock
125 g/4 oz fresh squid, cut into rings
125 g/4 oz salmon steak, boned and cubed
50 g/2 oz fresh or frozen cooked peeled prawns, thawed
salt and pepper
1 tablespoon chopped fresh fennel fronds, to garnish

**1** Bring at least 1.8 litres/3 pints water to the boil in a large saucepan. Add a dash of oil and a generous pinch of salt. Cook the pasta for 8–12 minutes.

**2** Meanwhile, melt the butter in a saucepan, stir in the flour and cook for about 1 minute. Gradually add the wine and the stock, whisking or beating the sauce over a moderate heat until thickened. Add salt and pepper to taste, stir in the squid, salmon and prawns, then simmer for 5 minutes.

**3** Drain the pasta and return it to the clean saucepan. Add the fish sauce and toss lightly. Serve at once, garnished with the fennel fronds.

**Serves 4**
Preparation time: 20 minutes
Cooking time: 12 minutes

# Tagliatelle with Garlic Mussels

- 1 tablespoon olive oil
- 300 g/10 oz dried tagliatelle
- 4 garlic cloves, crushed
- 1 kg/2 lb fresh mussels, scrubbed and bearded
- pinch of saffron strands
- 250 ml/8 fl oz double cream
- 2 tablespoons chopped fresh dill
- salt and pepper
- dill sprigs, to garnish

**1** Bring at least 1.8 litres/3 pints water to the boil in a large saucepan. Add a dash of oil and a pinch of salt. Cook the pasta for about 8–12 minutes, until just tender.

**2** Heat the remaining olive oil in a large saucepan. Add the crushed garlic and fry over a gentle heat for 3 minutes, stirring constantly, until softened, do not allow it to burn.

**3** Check over the fresh mussels carefully. Discard any which are open and do not close immediately when tapped on a work surface.

**4** Pound the saffron strands to a powder, and stir in 2–3 tablespoons of boiling water until dissolved. Stir into the cooked garlic in the saucepan, add the prepared mussels, cover and simmer for 5 minutes or until all the mussel shells have opened. Discard any mussels with shells which remain shut.

**5** Using a slotted spoon, remove the cooked mussels from the pan. Set aside 10 whole mussels for the garnish. Remove the remaining mussels from their shells and return them to the pan. Add the double cream and chopped fresh dill, with salt and pepper to taste. Simmer for 3 minutes.

**6** Drain the tagliatelle well and add it to the mussel sauce in the saucepan. Toss together well to mix.

**7** Serve the tagliatelle garnished with the reserved whole mussels in their shells and dill sprigs.

**Serves 4**
Preparation time: 30 minutes
Cooking time: 15 minutes

# Fusilli with Smoked Trout and Marsala

Smoked trout fillet is now widely available in larger supermarkets and has a delicious flavour which works well with this dish.

- 1 tablespoon olive oil
- 300 g/10 oz dried fusilli
- 1 garlic clove, crushed
- 2 shallots, chopped finely
- 1 tablespoon chopped fresh parsley
- 6 tablespoons Marsala
- 6 tablespoons single cream
- 1 x 230 g/7½ oz packet smoked trout fillet, broken into bite-sized pieces
- grated rind of 1 lemon
- salt and pepper
- 1 tablespoon chopped fresh parsley to garnish

**1** Bring at least 1.8 litres/3 pints water to the boil in a large saucepan. Add a dash of olive oil and a generous pinch of salt. Cook the dried fusilli for 8–12 minutes, until just tender.

**2** Meanwhile, heat the remaining oil in a saucepan and fry the crushed garlic and chopped shallots for 3 minutes until softened.

**3** Add the chopped parsley, Marsala and cream, stir well and season with salt and pepper to taste.

**4** Carefully fold in the smoked trout pieces and the grated lemon rind; gently heat through without allowing the mixture to boil.

**5** Drain the pasta well and return it to the clean saucepan. Add the smoked trout sauce to the pan and stir carefully.

**6** Serve at once, garnished with chopped fresh parsley.

**Serves 4**
Preparation time: 20 minutes
Cooking time: 12 minutes

# Char-grilled Cod Steaks with Fettuccine

- 4 cod steaks, about 150 g/5 oz each
- 4 tablespoons olive oil
- 1 teaspoon lime juice
- 1 teaspoon soy sauce
- 300 g/10 oz dried fettuccine
- 2 tablespoons chopped fresh flat leaf parsley
- salt and pepper

TO GARNISH:
- lemon wedges
- lime wedges
- flat leaf parsley sprigs

**1** Prepare a barbecue; alternatively, heat a griddle pan or non-stick frying pan. Brush each cod steak with a little oil. Drizzle over a little lime juice and soy sauce.

**2** Cook the fish on a grill over hot coals, on the griddle, or in the frying pan for about 8 minutes on each side, or until cooked through.

**3** Meanwhile, bring at least 1.8 litres/3 pints water to the boil in a large saucepan. Add a dash of oil and a generous pinch of salt. Cook the pasta for 8–12 minutes, until just tender.

**4** Drain the fettuccine and return it to the clean pan. Add the chopped fresh parsley, and stir, then drizzle over a little more olive oil, if liked. Season with salt and pepper and toss well. Spoon the fettuccine on to heated plates and serve with the char-grilled fish. Garnish with wedges of lemon and lime, and sprigs of flat leaf parsley.

**Serves 4**
Preparation time: 10 minutes
Cooking time: 16 minutes

# Gnocchi Fish Bake

- 500 g/1 lb Cyprus potatoes, peeled
- 1 egg, beaten
- 150 g/5 oz plain flour, sifted
- a little olive oil, see method
- chopped parsley, to garnish

FILLING:

- a few saffron strands
- 300 ml/½ pint hot fish stock
- 50 g/2 oz butter
- 50 g/2 oz plain flour
- 250 g/8 oz cooked peeled prawns
- 125 g/4 oz salmon steak, skinned and cubed
- 125 g/4 oz cod steak, skinned and cubed
- 4 tablespoons double cream
- 2 tablespoons chopped fresh dill
- salt and pepper

**1** Cook the potatoes in a saucepan of boiling water for 30 minutes or until tender enough to mash. Drain well and return to the pan. Mash the potatoes, then return the pan to a low heat to allow any excess liquid to evaporate. Beat in the egg and flour until smooth, then turn the mixture out on to a floured board. Shape into walnut-sized balls.

**2** Bring at least 1.8 litres/3 pints water to the boil in a large saucepan. Add a dash of oil and a pinch of salt. Cook the gnocchi, in 2 batches if necessary, for 3 minutes or until they all start to float to the surface. Drain well and keep hot.

**3** Make the filling. In a small bowl, pound the saffron to a powder then dissolve in a little fish stock. Melt the butter in a saucepan. Stir in the flour and cook for 1 minute. Gradually whisk or beat in the saffron, with the remaining fish stock, over a moderate heat for 5 minutes, until thickened. Season to taste.

**4** Carefully stir the prawns, salmon and cod into the sauce, with the cream and dill, then spoon into a 1.2 litre/2 pint ovenproof dish.

**5** Arrange the gnocchi over the fish, overlapping them slightly. Bake in a preheated oven, 180°C (350°F), Gas Mark 4, for 30 minutes. Serve garnished with chopped parsley.

**Serves 4**

Preparation time: 45 minutes
Cooking time: 1 hour 10 minutes
Oven temperature: 180°C (350°F), Gas Mark 4

# Seafood Linguine

FOR THE MARINADE:

- 2 tablespoons sun-dried tomato paste
- 2 teaspoons clear honey
- salt
- 2 teaspoons Chinese Five Spice Powder
- 2 tablespoons light soy sauce
- squeeze of lemon juice
- 1 teaspoon olive oil

FOR THE SKEWERS:

- 12 raw tiger prawns, shelled and deveined
- 250 g/8 oz salmon fillet, skinned and cut into chunks
- 1 teaspoon olive oil
- 500 g/1 lb packet fresh linguine verde
- 25 g/1 oz butter
- 2 shallots, finely chopped
- 300 ml/½ pint carton thick single cream
- salt and pepper
- spring onion, shredded, to garnish

**1** Put the marinade ingredients into a non-metallic bowl. Stir well, adding a little more lemon juice if the paste is too thick.

**2** Thread the tiger prawns and salmon onto 4 metal or soaked wooden skewers. Brush with just enough marinade to coat the fish lightly. Grill under a high heat for 5–7 minutes, brushing with marinade when you rotate the skewers.

**3** Meanwhile, bring at least 1.8 litres/3 pints water to the boil. Add the oil and a good pinch of salt. Add the linguine and cook for 4 minutes.

**4** Heat the butter in a frying pan, add the shallots and fry for 1 minute. Scrape any remaining marinade into the pan and heat gently. Add a little water to the hot marinade mixture if it starts to stick, stir well and then stir in the cream. Season well and simmer for 2 minutes. Drain the pasta. Return to the saucepan and pour in the hot sauce. Toss well. Spoon into the bowls and top with skewers. Garnish with shredded spring onion.

**Serves 4**

Preparation time: 25 minutes
Cooking time: 10 minutes

VARIATION

Omit the marinade and brush the skewers with oil and lime juice. Toss the pasta in melted butter with plenty of fresh dill.

# Tuna Stuffed Cannelloni

- 8 dried cannelloni tubes

FILLING:

- 1 x 200 g/7 oz can tuna fish in brine, drained
- 125 g/4 oz ricotta cheese
- 1 bunch watercress, trimmed and leaves chopped
- ½ teaspoon cayenne pepper
- 2 eggs, beaten
- salt and pepper

SAUCE:

- 15 g/½ oz butter
- 15 g/½ oz plain flour
- 300 ml/½ pint skimmed milk
- 125 g/4 oz Cheddar cheese, grated

**1** Make the filling, combine the tuna, ricotta, watercress, cayenne and eggs in a bowl. Add salt and pepper to taste and mash the mixture with a fork until smooth.

**2** Spoon a little of the filling into each cannelloni tube. Arrange the filled tubes in a single layer over the base of an oval or rectangular 1.8 litre/3 pint ovenproof dish, making sure that the cannelloni tubes just touch. Set aside.

**3** Make the sauce, melt the butter in a saucepan, stir in the flour and cook for 1 minute. Gradually add the milk, whisking or beating the sauce over a moderate heat until thickened.

**4** Stir in the Cheddar cheese until melted, and add salt and pepper to taste. Pour the sauce over the cannelloni tubes. Bake in a preheated oven, 180°C (350°F), Gas Mark 4, for 45 minutes until golden.

## Serves 4

Preparation time: 20 minutes
Cooking time: 45 minutes
Oven temperature: 180°C (350°F), Gas Mark 4

## Spaghetti with Anchovies and Olives

- oil, see method
- 375 g/12 oz dried spaghetti
- 25 g/1 oz butter
- 6 drained canned anchovy fillets, chopped
- 1 tablespoon tomato purée
- 1 tablespoon olive paste
- 6 pitted black olives, chopped
- salt and pepper
- bunch of fresh basil
- Parmesan shavings, to garnish

**1** Bring at least 1.8 litres/3 pints water to the boil in a large saucepan. Add a dash of oil and a generous pinch of salt. Cook the pasta for 8–12 minutes, until just tender.

**2** Drain the pasta and set it aside. Melt the butter in a large saucepan. Add the anchovy fillets, tomato purée, olive paste and olives. Stir over the heat until the mixture sizzles. Season well with pepper. Cool for 1 minute.

**3** Add the drained pasta to the saucepan. Toss well. Tear the basil leaves and add them to the pasta. Serve with shavings of Parmesan.

**Serves 4**
Preparation time: 10 minutes
Cooking time: 12–14 minutes

VARIATIONS

## Spaghetti with Tomato and Mussels

Make as for the main recipe, but add 250 g/8 oz chopped fresh plum tomatoes and substitute about 50 g/2 oz drained canned mussels for the anchovies. Add 1 tablespoon each of chopped fresh parsley and oregano instead of the torn basil leaves when tossing the pasta with the sauce.

## Spaghetti with Anchovies, Pesto and Balsamic Vinegar

Make as for the main recipe, omitting the olive paste and olives and adding 2 tablespoons of ready-made green or red pesto and 1 tablespoon balsamic vinegar to the anchovies and tomato purée. Stir in 1 red pepper (cored, deseeded and chopped). Continue as for the main recipe, and serve sprinkled with torn basil leaves and some shavings of Parmesan and a mixed salad, if you wish.

# Lasagne Marinara

Lasagne is the wide strip pasta used in baked dishes, and is widely used in Neapolitan cooking. It is available plain or in green, which has been flavoured with spinach – and also with straight of frilled edges. This recipe is for a seafood lasagne and uses the 'no pre-cook' variety, which has made life very much easier for the pasta cook.

- 9 dried 'no pre-cook' lasagne sheets
- 2 eggs, beaten
- 200 g/7 oz Cheddar cheese, grated
- sprigs of dill, to garnish

SAUCE:

- 50 g/2 oz butter
- 50 g/2 oz plain flour
- 600 ml/1 pint milk
- a few saffron strands
- 250 g/8 oz fresh salmon tail
- 125 g/4 oz cod fillet
- 125 g/4 oz fresh squid rings
- salt and pepper

**1** Make the sauce. Melt the butter in a saucepan, stir in the flour and cook for 1 minute. Gradually add the milk, whisking or beating the sauce over a moderate heat until it thickens. Pound the saffron strands to a powder in a bowl and stir in 2–3 tablespoons boiling water until dissolved. Add to the sauce, with salt and pepper to taste. Mix well.

**2** Remove any bones from the salmon and cod and cut the fish into bite-sized pieces. Fold the fish into the sauce with the squid rings. Remove from the heat.

**3** Spoon one-third of the fish mixture over the base of a 1.8 litre/3 pint ovenproof dish, and then cover with a layer of lasagne sheets. Repeat these layers twice, finishing with a layer of pasta sheets.

**4** Beat the eggs and Cheddar cheese together in a bowl. Add salt and pepper to taste and pour over the top of the lasagne.

**5** Bake in a preheated oven at 190°C (375°F), Gas Mark 5, for 45 minutes, covering the dish with foil after 30 minutes if the surface starts to overbrown. Serve, garnished with sprigs of dill.

**Serves 4**

Preparation time: 20 minutes
Cooking time: 45 minutes
Oven temperature: 190°C (375°F), Gas Mark 5

# Vegetarian Pasta

## Pasta-packed Baked Red Peppers

4 red peppers, halved, cored and deseeded

125 g/4 oz mini macaroni, cooked

2 plum tomatoes, chopped

125 g/4 oz Cheddar cheese, grated

2 spring onions, chopped finely

2 tablespoons chopped fresh parsley

3 tablespoons olive oil

salt and pepper

**1** Place the peppers on a baking sheet with the hollows uppermost. Mix the macaroni, tomatoes, cheese, spring onions and chopped parsley in a bowl. Spoon into the peppers, drizzle with plenty of olive oil and add salt and pepper to taste.

**2** Bake in a preheated oven, 180°C (350°F), Gas Mark 4, for 35–45 minutes or until the filling is golden and bubbling.

**3** Serve at once, with fresh crusty bread.

**Serves 4**

Preparation time: 20 minutes

Cooking time: 45 minutes

Oven temperature: 180°C (350°F), Gas Mark 4

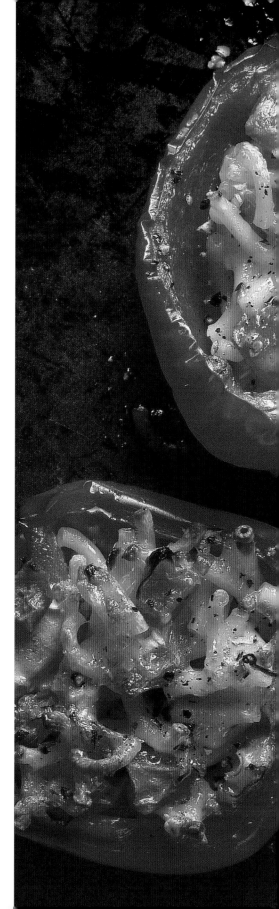

# Vegetable Bolognese

A vegetarian version of the classic Spaghetti Bolognese.

- 1 tablespoon olive oil
- 300 g/10 oz dried spaghetti verde
- 1 onion, chopped
- 1 x 200 g/7 oz can baby carrots, drained and diced
- 1 leek, trimmed, cleaned and sliced
- 2 celery sticks, sliced
- 1 x 425 g/14 oz can plum tomatoes, drained and roughly chopped
- 1 tablespoon tomato purée
- 1 teaspoon cayenne pepper
- 125 g/4 oz chestnut mushrooms, sliced
- salt and pepper
- basil leaves, to garnish

**1** Bring at least 1.8 litres/3 pints water to the boil in a large saucepan. Add a dash of oil and a generous pinch of salt. Cook the spaghetti verde for about 8–12 minutes, until just tender.

**2** Meanwhile, heat the remaining oil in a saucepan. Add the onion and fry over a low heat for 3–5 minutes, until softened. Add the carrots, leek and celery. Stir in the tomatoes, tomato purée, cayenne and mushrooms. Add salt and pepper to taste and simmer for 10 minutes.

**3** Drain the spaghetti and return it to the clean pan. Add black pepper to taste. Using a large fork, roll bundles of the pasta into 4 nests. Place 1 nest on each heated serving plate. Spoon one-quarter of the bolognese sauce into each nest. Arrange the basil leaves around the nests to garnish and serve immediately.

**Serves 4**
Preparation time: 15 minutes
Cooking time: 12 minutes

# Asparagus and Mushroom Tagliatelle

- 250 g/8 oz fresh asparagus spears, cut into 2.5 cm/1 inch lengths, blanched
- 125 g/4 oz chestnut mushrooms, sliced
- 2.5 cm/1 inch piece of fresh root ginger, grated
- 25 g/1 oz butter
- 1 tablespoon chopped fresh tarragon
- 250 ml/8 fl oz double cream or crème fraîche.
- oil, see method

- 300 g/10 oz fresh tagliatelle
- salt and pepper

TO GARNISH:
- sprigs of parsley (optional)
- strips of lemon rind

1 Place the asparagus, mushrooms, ginger and butter into a large frying pan and mix. Gently melt the butter and allow the vegetables to cook slowly, without browning, for about 5–8 minutes.

2 Add the tarragon and cream or crème fraîche to the pan, with salt and pepper to taste. Stir, then simmer for 5 minutes.

3 Bring at least 1.8 litres/3 pints water to the boil in a large saucepan. Add a dash of oil and a generous pinch of salt. Cook the pasta for 4–6 minutes or until it rises to the surface of the boiling water.

4 Drain the pasta and return it to the clean saucepan, pour the asparagus and mushroom sauce over the tagliatelle and stir carefully. Garnish with parsley, if liked and a few strips of lemon rind.

**Serves 4**
Preparation time: 10 minutes
Cooking time: 20 minutes

# Baked Stuffed Mushrooms

- 4 large field mushrooms
- 1 small onion, very finely chopped
- 50 g/2 oz mini macaroni, cooked
- 25 g/1 oz walnuts, chopped
- 1 tablespoon chopped fresh parsley
- 25 g/1 oz Cheddar cheese, cubed
- 1 tablespoon tomato purée
- 1 egg, beaten
- 1 tablespoon olive oil
- salt and pepper
- lemon wedges, to garnish

**1** Chop the mushroom stalks finely and set aside. Peel the mushrooms if blemished, and grill for 5 minutes until just softened. Remove and set aside.
**2** Put the chopped onion into a large bowl. Add the chopped mushroom stalks, cooked macaroni, walnuts, parsley, cheese and tomato purée. Mix well, and then add enough of the beaten egg to bind the mixture. Add salt and pepper to taste.
**3** Divide the filling between the mushrooms, mounding the mixture up with a spoon. Drizzle over a little olive oil. Arrange the filled mushrooms, well apart on a grill pan.
**4** Grill for 15–20 minutes until the top of the stuffing is crisp and has started to char at the edges, then serve, garnished with lemon wedges.

**Serves 4**
Preparation time: 10 minutes
Cooking time: 20 minutes

# Pesto Trapanese

This recipe is a legacy of the Arab domination of Sicily. The Arabs brought almonds to the island, and this pesto comes from Trapani, where they first settled. It really is a taste from the past, yet well suited to today's cooking. It is very garlicky.

- 500–750 g/1–1½ lb dried fusilli
- 3 ripe tomatoes
- 4 garlic cloves
- 50 g/2 oz basil leaves, plus extra to garnish
- 125 g/4 oz blanched almonds, toasted
- 150 ml/¼ pint olive oil
- salt and pepper

1 Bring at least 2 litres/3½ pints water to the boil in a large saucepan. Add a pinch of salt. Cook the pasta for 8–12 minutes or according to packet instructions.

2 Meanwhile, place all the remaining ingredients in a food processor and blend until smooth. Alternatively, finely chop the tomatoes, garlic, basil and almonds by hand and stir in the olive oil, to give a chunkier sauce. Season to taste with salt and pepper.

3 Toss the pesto with the cooked pasta. The pesto is warmed by the heat of the pasta. Garnish with a few basil leaves.

**Serves 4–6**
Preparation time: 12 minutes
Cooking time: 8–12 minutes

# Aubergine Layer Bake

- 2 aubergines, sliced
- 25 g/1 oz salt
- 2 tablespoons olive oil
- 1 onion, chopped
- 1 tablespoon chopped fresh oregano
- 1 tablespoon chopped fresh basil
- 125 g/4 oz button mushrooms, cut into quarters
- 1 x 550 g/18 oz jar passata (sieved tomatoes)
- 8–9 fresh lasagne sheets
- 375 g/12 oz mozzarella cheese, sliced
- 125 g/4 oz Gruyère cheese, grated
- salt and pepper

**1** Spread out the aubergine slices on baking sheets. Sprinkle with the salt and set aside for 15 minutes.

**2** Heat 1 tablespoon of the oil in a large frying pan. Add the onion; fry for 3–5 minutes, stirring until softened. Add the herbs, mushrooms and passata. Simmer for 10 minutes, then add salt and pepper to taste.

**3** Rinse the aubergine slices under plenty of cold water, drain and pat dry with paper towels.

**4** Spread the aubergine slices on baking sheets. Brush with the remaining oil. Grill under a high heat for 10 minutes, turning once. Remove from the heat.

**5** Arrange 3 lasagne sheets on the base of a lightly greased rectangular 1.2 litre/2 pint ovenproof dish. Spoon over one-third of the tomato sauce. Place a layer of aubergines on top, and add one-third of the mozzarella and Gruyère cheese.

**6** Repeat the layers twice more. Cover with foil. Bake in a preheated oven, 190°C (375°F), Gas Mark 5, for 45 minutes. Remove the foil after 20 minutes to allow the top to brown and the cheese to melt completely.

## Serves 4

Preparation time: 30 minutes
Cooking time: 50 minutes
Oven temperature: 190°C (375°F), Gas Mark 5

# Deep-fried Camembert with Fettuccine

- 8 Camembert wedges, chilled
- 2 eggs, beaten
- 125 g/4 oz fresh wholemeal breadcrumbs
- 1 teaspoon paprika
- oil, for deep frying
- 300 g/10 oz fresh fettuccine
- 1 tablespoon olive oil
- 1 tablespoon raspberry vinegar
- salt and pepper

TO GARNISH:
- fresh raspberries
- raspberry leaves

**1** Dip the Camembert wedges in egg, then in breadcrumbs to coat completely. Sprinkle with paprika and chill the wedges on a plate for 30 minutes.

**2** Bring at least 1.8 litres/3 pints water to the boil in a large saucepan. Add a dash of oil and a generous pinch of salt. Cook the pasta for about 8–12 minutes or until just tender.

**3** Heat the oil for deep frying to 180-190°C (350-375°F) – or until a cube of bread browns in 30 seconds. Fry the Camembert wedges for 1 minute, turning once. Drain on paper towels and keep hot.

**4** Drain the pasta and return to the clean saucepan. Add the oil and vinegar and season to taste. Toss well, twirl into 4 nests and place on heated serving plates. Add 2 deep-fried Camembert wedges to each portion. Garnish with raspberries and raspberry leaves and serve red-currant jelly separately, if liked.

**Serves 4**
Preparation time: 10 minutes
Cooking time: 12 minutes

# Sun-dried Tomato Pappardelle

- 3 tablespoons olive oil
- 375 g/12 oz dried pappardelle or other broad egg noodles
- 2 tablespoons chopped fresh basil
- 2 tablespoons chopped fresh oregano
- 12 sun-dried tomatoes in oil, drained and chopped
- salt and pepper
- 50 g/2 oz fresh Parmesan cheese, to serve

**1** Bring at least 1.8 litres/3 pints water to the boil in a large saucepan. Add a dash of oil and a generous pinch of salt. Cook the pasta for 8–12 minutes, until just tender.
**2** Pour the olive oil into a large saucepan. Add the basil, oregano and sun-dried tomatoes. Cook over a low heat for 3 minutes, stirring constantly.
**3** Drain the pasta and return to the clean pan. Drizzle with a little olive oil and add plenty of black pepper to taste. Pour the sun-dried tomato sauce over the pasta, toss well and spoon on to heated plates. Serve with shavings of Parmesan.

**Serves 4**
Preparation time: 10 minutes
Cooking time: 12 minutes

# Pasta with Ginger and Carrot Ribbons

A light yet flavoursome dish – sautéeing the carrot and ginger adds a buttery finish to the pasta.

- 300 g/10 oz dried pappardelle or other broad egg noodles
- 2 carrots
- 25 g/1 oz butter (optional)
- 2.5 cm/1 inch piece fresh root ginger, grated
- 2 tablespoons olive oil
- 25 g/1 oz pine nuts
- salt and pepper

**1** Bring at least 1.8 litres/3 pints water to the boil in a large saucepan. Add a dash of oil and a generous pinch of salt. Cook the pasta for 8–12 minutes, until just tender.
**2** Meanwhile, using a potato peeler, make shavings of carrot ribbons.
**3** Either melt the butter in a frying pan and sauté the carrot and ginger for 5 minutes or steam them without the butter until tender.
**4** Drain the pasta and return it to the clean pan. Toss with olive oil and season with black pepper.
**5** Carefully fold the carrot mixture into the cooked pasta. Sprinkle with pine nuts and serve.

**Serves 4**
Preparation time: 10 minutes
Cooking time: 12 minutes

# Cambozola with Campanelli and Walnuts

- 2 tablespoons olive oil
- 300 g/10 oz dried egg campanelli
- 2 garlic cloves, crushed
- 3 tablespoons ready-made red pesto
- 300 ml/½ pint double cream
- 125 g/4 oz Cambozola cheese, crumbled
- 125 g/4 oz walnuts, halved
- 2 tablespoons chopped fresh basil
- salt and pepper

**1** Bring at least 1.8 litres/3 pints water to the boil in a large saucepan. Add a dash of oil and a generous pinch of salt. Cook the pasta for 8–12 minutes, until just tender.

**2** Meanwhile, heat 1 tablespoon of the remaining oil in a saucepan. Fry the garlic over a gentle heat for 3 minutes until softened. Remove from the heat. Cool slightly, then stir in the pesto and cream.

**3** Drain the pasta and return it to the clean pan. Add the garlic mixture with the cheese and walnuts. Toss to mix, then add salt and pepper to taste. Add the basil, toss again and serve. A tossed leaf salad makes an excellent accompaniment.

**Serves 4**
Preparation time: 10 minutes
Cooking time: 12 minutes

# Spaghetti with Marinated Vegetables

- 1 red pepper, coredand deseeded
- 1 tablespoon salt
- 1 small aubergine, sliced
- 125 g/4 oz flat field mushrooms
- 1 leek, trimmed, cleaned and sliced thinly
- 1 teaspoon cumin seeds
- ½ teaspoon coriander seeds
- 150 ml/¼ pint raspberry vinegar
- 300 ml/½ pint olive oil
- 1 tablespoon garlic purée
- 300 g/10 oz dried spaghetti
- salt and pepper

TO GARNISH:
- mixed salad leaves
- flat leaf parsley

**1** Place the red pepper halves on a grill pan, skin side up, and grill under a high heat for about 10 minutes until the skin has blackened and blistered. Remove from the heat and leave to cool.

**2** Meanwhile, sprinkle the salt over the aubergine slices and set aside for 15 minutes. Drain the aubergine slices, rinse them well and pat dry with paper towels. Place on a grill pan, and grill under a high heat for 10 minutes, turning the slices once, until browned. Remove from the grill pan and set aside.

**3** Add the mushrooms to the grill pan and grill for 2 minutes.

**4** Peel the pepper and finely slice the flesh. Slice the mushrooms. Combine the all grilled vegetables in a large bowl and add the leek. Stir in the spices, vinegar, oil and garlic purée with salt and pepper to taste. Toss the mixture until combined, and set aside.

**5** Bring at least 1.8 litres/3 pints water to the boil in a large saucepan. Add a dash of oil and a generous pinch of salt. Cook the pasta for 8–12 minutes, until just tender. Drain thoroughly and add to the vegetable mixture. Toss again and chill for 3 hours before serving.

**6** Serve garnished with salad leaves and flat leaf parsley.

### Serves 4
Preparation time: 20 minutes
Cooking time: 20 minutes, plus 3 hours chilling time

# Three Cheese Rigatoni

Substitute vegetarian cheeses made without the use of animal rennet if preferred.

- 1 tablespoon olive oil
- 375 g/12 oz dried rigatoni
- 1 red-skinned onion, sliced
- 125 g/4 oz button mushrooms, sliced
- 1 courgette, trimmed and grated
- 125 g/4 oz Cheddar cheese, grated
- 125 g/4 oz Pecorino cheese, grated
- 125 g/4 oz Emmental cheese, grated
- salt and pepper
- mixed fresh herbs, to garnish

**1** Bring at least 1.8 litres/3 pints water to the boil in a large saucepan. Add a dash of oil and a generous pinch of salt. Cook the pasta for 8–12 minutes, until just tender.
**2** Meanwhile, heat the remaining oil in a frying pan and fry the onion for 3–5 minutes or until softened. Add the mushrooms and courgette. Fry for a further 3 minutes. Add salt and pepper to taste.
**3** Drain the pasta. Spoon half of it into a lightly greased 1.8 litre/3 pint ovenproof dish. Spoon over half the mushroom mixture and half the mixed cheeses. Spread the remaining pasta on top, followed by the rest of the mushroom mixture, and lastly the remaining mixed cheeses.
**4** Cover the dish with foil and bake in a preheated oven, 190°C (375°F), Gas Mark 5, for 35 minutes, removing the foil after 20 minutes to allow the top to go golden brown in colour. Garnish with plenty of fresh herbs and serve hot with some crusty garlic bread.

**Serves 4**
Preparation time: 10 minutes
Cooking time: 35 minutes
Oven temperature: 190°C (375°F), Gas Mark 5

# Pasta Salads

## Three-bean Pasta Twist Salad

oil, see method

300 g/10 oz dried tricolore pasta twists

2 spring onions, chopped diagonally

1 red pepper, cored, seeded and chopped

125 g/4 oz drained canned red kidney beans

125 g/4 oz drained canned pinto beans

125 g/4 oz drained canned borlotti beans

200 ml/7 fl oz crème fraîche

4 tablespoons milk

3 tablespoons chopped fresh dill

salt and pepper

dill sprigs, to garnish

**1** Bring at least 1.8 litres/3 pints water to the boil in a large saucepan. Add a dash of oil and a generous pinch of salt. Cook the pasta for 8–12 minutes, until just tender. Drain the pasta, then rinse under cold water in a colander; drain again and transfer to a large salad bowl.

**2** Add the spring onions, red pepper and beans. Mix well. Beat the crème fraîche and milk together in a bowl; fold into the salad and add salt and freshly ground black pepper to taste.

**3** Fold in the dill and serve, garnished with sprigs of dill.

**Serves 4**

Preparation time: 20 minutes

Cooking time: 12 minutes

# Shellfish Cocktail Salad

- oil, see method
- pinch salt
- 250 g/8 oz small dried pasta shells
- ½ iceberg lettuce, shredded
- 50 g/2 oz cooked peeled prawns
- 50 g/2 oz cockles in vinegar, drained
- 3 rollmop herrings, finely sliced
- 1 tablespoon tomato purée
- 4 tablespoons light mayonnaise
- 1 teaspoon mild chilli powder
- 2 teaspoons lemon juice
- parsley sprigs, to garnish

**1** Bring at least 1.8 litres/3 pints water to the boil in a large saucepan. Add a dash of oil and a generous pinch of salt. Cook the pasta for 8–12 minutes, until just tender. Drain the pasta, rinse under cold water in a colander and drain again.

**2** Divide the lettuce between 4 individual glass bowls. In a mixing bowl combine the cooked pasta with the prawns, cockles and herrings. Stir carefully to mix.

**3** In another bowl mix the tomato purée, mayonnaise, chilli powder and lemon juice. Spoon into the pasta mixture and toss lightly to coat.

**4** Spoon the shellfish cocktail over the lettuce. Chill in the refrigerator until ready to serve. Garnish with parsley before serving.

**Serves 4**
Preparation time: 10 minutes
Cooking time: 12 minutes

# Mexican Pasta Salad

- oil, see method
- 300 g/10 oz dried conchigliette rigate
- 2 ripe avocados, halved, stones removed
- 8 tablespoons soured cream
- 3 teaspoons chilli sauce
- 2 tablespoons lime juice
- 250 g/8 oz drained canned red kidney beans
- salt and pepper

TO GARNISH:

1 tablespoon parsley leaves
- cayenne pepper

**1** Bring at least 1.8 litres/3 pints water to the boil in a large saucepan. Add a dash of oil and a generous pinch of salt. Cook the pasta for about 8–12 minutes, until just tender.
**2** Drain the pasta, rinse under cold running water in a colander, drain again and transfer to a large bowl.
**3** Put the avocado flesh in a food processor or bowl. Add the soured cream, chilli sauce and lime juice. Process for 1 minute. Alternatively, mash the avocado with a fork and then stir the remaining ingredients into the avocado.
**4** Spoon the avocado sauce over the pasta and stir well. Add salt and pepper to taste and the kidney beans, toss and serve, sprinkled with cayenne pepper and parsley leaves.

**Serves 4**
Preparation time: 10 minutes
Cooking time: 12 minutes

# Crunchy Pasta Salad

- oil, see method
- 300 g/10 oz dried pasta shells
- ¼ red cabbage, shredded
- 2 celery sticks, chopped
- 1 Granny Smith apple, cored
- 1 tablespoon lemon juice
- 25 g/1 oz sultanas
- 4 tablespoons mayonnaise
- 4 tablespoons semi-skimmed milk
- salt and pepper

TO GARNISH:

- pinch of cayenne pepper
- celery leaves

**1** Bring at least 1.8 litres/3 pints water to the boil in a large saucepan. Add a dash of oil and a generous pinch of salt. Cook the pasta for 8–12 minutes, until just tender.
**2** Drain the pasta and rinse under cold running water in a colander. Drain again thoroughly and transfer to a large salad bowl.
**3** Add the cabbage and celery. Quarter the apple and slice it into a bowl. Sprinkle with lemon juice to prevent the apple from browning.
**4** Fold the apple slices into the pasta with the sultanas. Mix together the mayonnaise and milk, add salt and pepper to taste, and fold into the salad. Garnish with the cayenne pepper and celery leaves.

## Serves 4
Preparation time: 20 minutes
Cooking time: 12 minutes

# Tuna Pasta Shell Salad

One of the very best pasta salads – equally good with cooked fresh tuna, especially if it has been barbecued. The combination of tuna, walnuts and pesto also makes a very good sauce with hot pasta too.

- 4 tablespoons olive oil
- 400 g/13 oz fresh pasta shells
- 5 tablespoons ready-made pesto
- 1 teaspoon white wine vinegar
- 1 teaspoon grated lemon rind
- 1 x 200 g/7 oz can tuna in brine, drained and flaked
- 50 g/2 oz walnut pieces
- salt and pepper
- 6 large basil leaves, shredded

**1** Bring at least 1.8 litres/3 pints water to the boil in a large saucepan. Add a dash of oil and a generous pinch of salt. Cook the pasta shells for between 4–8 minutes, or until they all rise to the surface of the boiling water.

**2** Drain the pasta, rinse under cold running water in a colander and drain again. Transfer to a large salad bowl.

**3** Mix the pesto sauce and vinegar in a bowl. Season well with black pepper. Add to the pasta with the grated lemon rind and toss well.

**4** Fold the tuna and walnuts into the pasta. Sprinkle with the basil and drizzle the remaining olive oil over the top. Mix carefully, then serve immediately, or chill until required.

**Serves 4**
Preparation time: 10 minutes
Cooking time: about 8 minutes

# Broccoli and Red Pepper Fettuccine

- 6 tablespoons olive oil
- 300 g/10 oz fresh fettuccine
- 3 red peppers, cored, deseeded and halved
- 250 g/8 oz small broccoli florets
- 2 tablespoons balsamic vinegar
- salt and pepper
- basil leaves, to garnish

**1** Bring at least 1.8 litres/3 pints water to the boil in a large saucepan. Add a dash of oil and a pinch of salt. Cook the pasta for 4–6 minutes, until just tender.
**2** Drain, rinse under cold running water in a colander and drain again. Set aside in a large salad bowl.
**3** Grill the peppers, skin side up, until the skins have blackened and blistered. Remove from the heat and leave to cool for 5 minutes.
**4** Meanwhile, bring a large saucepan of lightly salted water to the boil and blanch the broccoli florets for 3 minutes. Drain, rinse under cold running water and drain again.
**5** Peel the peppers and slice the flesh into strips. Add to the pasta with the drained broccoli florets, remaining olive oil and the balsamic vinegar. Add salt and pepper to taste and toss well. Serve at once, garnished with basil leaves.

**Serves 4**
Preparation time: 10 minutes
Cooking time: about 15 minutes

VARIATIONS

# Chick Pea, Spinach and Mushroom Fettuccine

Make the salad as for the main recipe, omitting the broccoli. Substitute 125 g/4 oz drained canned chick peas, 25 g/1 oz torn young spinach leaves and 25 g/1 oz sliced mushrooms. Add the dressing and toss well, then serve with a little soured cream.

# Fettuccine Verde with Gorgonzola

Substitute green (verde) fettuccine for the plain pasta in the main recipe. Cook, drain and transfer to a salad bowl. Add the peppers but omit the broccoli when mixing the salad. Stir in 250 g/8 oz cubed Gorgonzola cheese. Use white wine vinegar instead of balsamic vinegar in the dressing and add 1 teaspoon Dijon mustard.

# Goats' Cheese and Watercress Conchiglie

- 6 tablespoons olive oil
- 300 g/10 oz dried conchiglie
- 3 spring onions, sliced diagonally
- 3 tablespoons raspberry vinegar
- 125 g/4 oz soft goats' cheese, diced
- 1 orange or grapefruit, peeled and sliced into rings
- 1 bunch watercress, washed and trimmed
- salt and pepper

**1** Bring 1.8 litres/3 pints water to the boil in a large saucepan. Add a dash of oil and a generous pinch of salt. Cook the pasta for about 8–12 minutes, until just tender.
**2** Drain the pasta, rinse under cold running water in a colander and drain again. Transfer to a large salad bowl.
**3** Mix the spring onions, raspberry vinegar and remaining oil in a bowl. Add salt and pepper to taste and pour over the pasta.
**4** Fold in the goats' cheese, the orange or grapefruit slices and the watercress. Toss and chill the salad until required.

**Serves 4**
Preparation time: 10 minutes
Cooking time: 12 minutes

# Herb Sausage and Garlic Penne Salad

- 250 g/8 oz herb pork sausages
- 4 tablespoons light olive oil
- 300 g/10 oz dried penne
- 1–2 garlic cloves, crushed
- 1 shallot, chopped finely
- 2 gherkins, chopped finely
- 1 tablespoon chopped fresh parsley
- salt and pepper
- 1 teaspoon chopped fresh parsley, to garnish

**1** Grill the sausages until cooked right through and crisp on the outside. Remove from the heat and cool for 10 minutes.

**2** Bring at least 1.8 litres/3 pints water to the boil in a large saucepan. Add a dash of oil and a pinch of salt. Cook the pasta for 8–12 minutes, until just tender.

**3** Drain the pasta, rinse under cold running water in a colander and drain again. Transfer to a large salad bowl. Mix the garlic, shallot, gherkins, remaining oil and parsley in a bowl. Add to the pasta with salt and pepper to taste; toss well.

**4** Cut the sausages into large chunks and stir them into the salad. Garnish with the chopped parsley. Serve immediately or chill until required.

**Serves 4**
Preparation time: 10 minutes
Cooking time: 25–35 minutes

# Chicken and Mushroom Penne Salad

- 300 g/10 oz fresh penne or dried wholewheat penne
- 3 tablespoons sesame oil
- 250 g/8 oz cooked chicken breast, sliced into strips
- 125 g/4 oz button mushrooms, sliced
- 1 red pepper, cored, deseeded and finely sliced
- 1 teaspoon sesame seeds
- 1 tablespoon lemon juice
- 4 spring onions, sliced diagonally
- salt and pepper
- 2 tablespoons chopped fresh parsley, to garnish

**1** Bring at least 1.8 litres/3 pints water to the boil in a large saucepan. Add a dash of oil and a generous pinch of salt. Cook fresh pasta for 4–8 minutes; dried pasta for 8–12 minutes. Drain the pasta, rinse under cold running water in a colander and drain again. Transfer to a large salad bowl.
**2** Add the chicken, mushrooms and red pepper, with the remaining oil, sesame seeds, lemon juice and spring onions. Add salt and pepper to taste and toss well. Garnish with the chopped fresh parsley.

**Serves 4**
Preparation time: 15 minutes
Cooking time: 8–12 minutes

VARIATIONS

# Chicken Salad with Avocado and Raspberry Vinegar

Make the salad as for the main recipe, omitting the lemon juice. Toss 1 sliced avocado in 2 tablespoons of raspberry vinegar. Season with plenty of black pepper. Add the avocado to the salad with 2 chopped plum tomatoes, or heap the salad on a large platter and arrange the avocado with plum tomato slices around the rim. Sprinkle a little chopped basil over the tomato.

# Spanish Sausage and Chicken Penne Salad

Cook the pasta as for the main recipe. Add the chicken and mushrooms but not the red pepper. Slice 2 chorizo sausages and add them to the salad with 1 sliced, deseeded green pepper. Omit the sesame oil and sesame seeds from the dressing; instead, whisk 2 tablespoons mild chilli sauce with the lemon juice and spring onions. Add salt and pepper to taste and toss well. Garnish with the chopped parsley as for the main recipe.

# Warm Italian Mix Salad

- 300 g/10 oz dried pasta wheels
- 1 red pepper, cored, deseeded and quartered
- 125 g/4 oz mozzarella cheese, grated
- 125 g/4 oz Red Leicester cheese, grated
- 50 g/2 oz salami slices, chopped
- 2 ripe plum tomatoes, chopped
- 50 g/2 oz pitted black olives
- 2 tablespoons lemon juice
- salt and pepper
- 1 tablespoon chopped fresh parsley, to garnish

**1** Bring at least 1.8 litres/3 pints water to the boil in a large saucepan. Add a dash of oil and a generous pinch of salt. Cook the pasta wheels for 8–12 minutes, until just tender.

**2** Meanwhile, place the red pepper in a grill pan, skin side uppermost. Grill under a high heat until the skin has blackened and blistered. Remove the pepper quarters from the heat and set aside to cool for 5 minutes.

**3** Drain the pasta in a colander and toss immediately with the grated cheeses. Transfer to a large salad bowl.

**4** Peel away the pepper skin. Slice the flesh and add to the pasta with the salami, tomatoes and black olives.

**5** Add the lemon juice, with salt and pepper to taste; toss well. Garnish with chopped parsley and serve immediately, while still warm.

**Serves 4**

Preparation time: 20 minutes
Cooking time: 12 minutes

**VARIATION**

Prepare as for the main recipe, replacing the mozzarella cheese and Red Leicester with goats' cheese or Roquefort. Replace the fresh parsley with large basil leaves.

# Balsamic Aubergine Salad

- 1 large aubergine, sliced
- 1 tablespoon salt
- 150 ml/¼ pint olive oil
- 300 g/10 oz dried penne rigate
- 6 tablespoons balsamic vinegar
- 1 teaspoon Dijon mustard
- 2 celery sticks, chopped
- 125 g/4 oz drained canned red kidney beans
- salt and pepper
- celery leaves, to garnish

**1** Spread out the aubergine slices on baking sheets and sprinkle with the salt. Set aside for 15 minutes.
**2** Meanwhile, bring at least 1.8 litres/ 3 pints water to the boil in a large saucepan. Add a dash of olive oil and a generous pinch of salt. Cook the pasta for 8–12 minutes, until it is just tender.
**3** Drain the pasta and rinse under cold running water in a colander. Drain again, transfer to a large salad bowl and set aside.
**4** Rinse the aubergines slices under plenty of cold water, drain and pat dry with paper towels. Grill under a high heat for 10 minutes until crisp, turning once. Slice some of the aubergine rounds in half. Set aside.
**5** In a bowl, whisk the olive oil with the vinegar and Dijon mustard. Add salt and pepper to taste. Add the dressing to the pasta and toss well. Fold in the celery and kidney beans, with the reserved aubergine slices. Garnish with celery leaves and serve at once.

### Serves 4
Preparation time: 20 minutes, plus 15 minutes standing time
Cooking time: 12 minutes

# Pasta Niçoise

- 300 g/10 oz dried pasta twists
- 250 g/8 oz French beans, trimmed, halved and cooked
- 25 g/1 oz anchovy fillets
- 2 teaspoons capers, chopped
- 25 g/1 oz pitted black olives
- 1 large ripe plum tomato, cut lengthways into eighths
- salt and pepper

DRESSING:
- 4 tablespoons olive oil
- 2 tablespoons sherry vinegar
- 1 teaspoon Dijon mustard
- pinch of sugar
- 1 tablespoon basil leaves, to garnish

**1** Bring at least 1.8 litres/ 3 pints water to the boil in a large saucepan. Add a dash of oil and a generous pinch of salt. Cook the pasta twists for 8–12 minutes, until just tender.

**2** Drain the pasta and rinse under cold running water in a colander. Drain again and set aside while preparing the salad.

**3** Place the French beans in a bowl with the anchovy fillets, capers, olives and tomato. Add plenty of salt and pepper to taste. Add the pasta and toss well.

**4** Make the dressing. Place the oil, vinegar, mustard and sugar in a screw-top jar. Close the jar tightly and shake well. Pour over the salad, toss again and sprinkle over the basil leaves. Chill in the refrigerator until required.

**Serves 4**
Preparation time: 20 minutes
Cooking time: 12 minutes

Recipe Photographer:
James Murphy
Recipe Home Economists:
Allyson Birch, Jane Stevenson and Janet Smith
Jacket Photographer:
Ian Wallace
Jacket Home Economist:
Louise Pickford